JANA RAE

Unbroken

A Memoir of Survival, Silence, and Finding Home Again

Copyright © 2025 by Jana Rae

All rights reserved. No part of this publication may be reproduced, stored or transmitted in any form or by any means, electronic, mechanical, photocopying, recording, scanning, or otherwise without written permission from the publisher. It is illegal to copy this book, post it to a website, or distribute it by any other means without permission.

This memoir is a true and factual account of the author's personal life experiences. All names, places, and events are represented as they occurred to the best of the author's memory. No names or identifying details have been changed.

The author has written this work with honesty and transparency, acknowledging that memories may be interpreted differently by others involved. This book is not intended to harm, defame, or misrepresent any individual or entity, but to share the author's lived truth.

The content is for storytelling and testimonial purposes only and does not constitute professional medical, psychological, or legal advice. Readers seeking support for trauma, mental illness, or abuse are encouraged to seek guidance from licensed professionals.

First edition

ISBN: 9798281207263

This book was professionally typeset on Reedsy.
Find out more at reedsy.com

Contents

Foreword	iv
Dedication	vi
Acknowledgments	vii
About the Author	ix
Before We Begin	x
Chapter One	1
Chapter 2	15
Chapter 3	26
Chapter 4	37
Chapter 5	55
Chapter 6	64
Chapter 7	79
Chapter 8	92
Chapter 9	108
Chapter 10	121
Chapter 11	135
Chapter 12	146
Chapter 13	159
Chapter 14	174
Closing Reflection	190

Foreword

If you're here, reading this, I just want to start by saying thank you. Thank you for picking up this book. Thank you for being willing to step into the mess and the beauty of my story. I won't lie to you—these pages hold a lot. Some of it is heavy. Some of it is hard. Some of it might make you stop and take a deep breath before you keep going. But it's real. And it's mine. And maybe—just maybe—parts of it will feel a little bit like yours too.

This isn't a book filled with tidy lessons or happy endings wrapped in bows. It's not polished or perfect. It's honest. It's raw. It's full of moments I didn't think I'd survive, and quiet mornings I never thought I'd see. It's about a little girl who was afraid of her own home. About growing up in a world where safety was something I had to imagine more than feel. It's about trauma and motherhood and mental illness and heartbreak. But it's also about hope. About healing. About love showing up when I least expected it, and how something as simple as baking bread or washing dishes slowly can become a lifeline when everything else feels like too much.

There were a lot of days I didn't think I'd make it here. Days I stayed in bed with the curtains closed. Days I checked the locks a hundred times. Days I felt like a ghost in my own life. But somehow, I kept waking up. Kept showing up. Kept trying. And eventually… I started healing.

This book is a collection of moments. Some are messy. Some are sacred. Some are just plain ordinary. But they're all pieces of my life. And I'm sharing them with you not because I've got it all figured out, but because maybe—if you've ever felt broken or tired or like the world has forgotten you—this will remind you that you're not alone.

I wrote this for the woman sitting in her kitchen at 2 a.m. staring into a cup of tea, wondering how she's still standing. For the ones who've been through things nobody knows about. For the quiet survivors. For the women who carry so much and still love deeply. For the ones who were told they weren't enough, and are just now starting to believe otherwise.

If you see yourself in any of these pages, I hope you'll keep reading. I hope you'll find comfort here. And more than anything, I hope this reminds you that even after everything—you can still build something soft and beautiful with what you have left.

With all my heart,
Jana

Dedication

To the girl I used to be—
the one who cried herself to sleep,
who checked every lock twice,
who thought she wouldn't make it.
You did.
You're still here.
And I'm so proud of you.

To Tim—
for loving me in the quiet,
for showing up and staying,
for never asking me to be anyone other than myself.
You brought peace where there was panic,
and laughter when I thought I'd forgotten how.

To every woman who has felt invisible,
unworthy, broken, or too far gone—
this is for you.
You are not alone.
There's still beauty left.
There's still hope.
And your story matters.

Acknowledgments

There are some stories that can't be written without a whole lot of grace, grit, and the people who held your hand—sometimes without even knowing they were doing it.

To **Tim**—

You walked into my life when I was shattered, and you never once asked me to be whole. Thank you for being patient with my silence, for understanding my fears, and for loving me exactly where I was. I will never stop being grateful that you stayed. I love you more now than I did that first day—and that's saying something.

To **my readers and viewers**, especially those who have followed my journey on *Home with Jana*—

Your messages, your kindness, and your willingness to show up and say "me too" made all the difference. Thank you for reminding me that sharing my story matters. You gave me the courage to speak, and I carry your hearts with mine.

To **those who left**—

Thank you. Your absence carved space for something better. Your rejection taught me boundaries. And your silence reminded me how to hear my own voice again.

To **my kitchen**—

Yes, the whole thing. The flour-covered counters, the steam on the windows, the playlist playing softly in the background. You cradled me when I couldn't bear to be seen. You became my therapy when words were too heavy. You gave me rhythm when my life had none.

To **God**—

You never stopped showing up, even when I was angry. Even when I was silent. Even when I couldn't feel You. Thank You for never leaving me, even in the darkest rooms, even on the hardest nights.

And finally, to **the woman I've become**—

You didn't quit. Not once. You cried, you broke, you curled up on the floor—but you always got back up. You kept loving. You kept baking. You kept believing—sometimes with the smallest flicker of faith—but it was enough. I see you now. I'm proud of you.

With love,

Jana

About the Author

Jana Rae is a storyteller, a homemaker, a survivor, and a woman who knows what it means to rise from the ashes more than once. She has spent a lifetime rebuilding herself from moments that nearly broke her—and learning how to find beauty in the quiet, comfort in the kitchen, and healing in the most ordinary places.

Diagnosed with PTSD, severe depressive disorder, bipolar disorder, and paranoid schizophrenia, Jana Rae has lived much of her life in survival mode. But through baking, prayer, creativity, and a deep yearning for peace, she found her way to solid ground. Her writing reflects her journey—not polished or perfect, but real, raw, and overflowing with grace.

She lives in Michigan with Tim, her best friend and partner of over a decade. Together, they've created a small, love-filled life that's built on trust, laughter, and homemade meals. When she's not writing, you'll find her painting, gardening, tending to her cozy kitchen, or sharing inspiration with others through her YouTube channel, *Home with Jana Show*.

This is the only memoir she ever plans to write—because some stories are so deep, so sacred, they only need to be told once.

Before We Begin

"Some things don't break.
They bend, they ache, they change shape...
but they don't break.
And neither did I."

This book isn't just a memoir—it's a patchwork quilt of all the moments that made me. The bruises and the breakthroughs. The silence and the cinnamon. The aching nights and the tender mornings that reminded me I was still here.

If you're holding this, maybe you know something about starting over. About surviving what you never thought you could. About becoming someone new on the other side of pain. If so, this story is for you.

I don't have all the answers. I'm still figuring it out. But I'm here. And that, all by itself, is something sacred.

So come sit with me. Pour a cup of tea. Let's begin—right where the world cracked open... and somehow, the light still came in.

With love,
Jana

Chapter One

Some of my earliest memories aren't soft ones. They aren't the kind of childhood moments people fondly bring up when flipping through old photo albums or watching home videos. Mine come with the smell of stale cigarettes and burnt coffee, the slam of a door too hard, the sound of my mother's voice breaking mid-sentence. I don't remember a time when fear wasn't part of me. It was there before I even had words for it—hiding under my bed, sitting beside me at dinner, brushing against my shoulders when I walked too quietly through the hallway.

Fear was like wallpaper in that house. Always there. Always pressing in.

People sometimes say children are resilient, that we bounce back easily from pain. But I think children are just quiet survivors. We don't always cry or scream—we learn how to go still. How to watch. How to shrink ourselves. I was little when I started shrinking. I don't even know how old, just that the sound of my father's voice could send my stomach into knots. He had a loud, wild kind of presence. The kind that made everything feel too big—his footsteps, his anger, his moods that shifted like storms. And when he exploded, nothing was safe. Not the furniture. Not the walls. Certainly not us.

I remember laying in bed some nights with the blanket pulled all the way up, even in the summer when it was too hot. The blanket didn't help, not really—but it was all I had. That and a stuffed animal with matted fur and one button eye, which I used to whisper to like it could actually hear me. I'd try to focus on the hum of the fan, the one in the hallway that made this low, whirring sound. I thought if I could focus hard enough on that sound, it might drown out the rest—the yelling, the breaking glass, my mother's voice trying to reason with a man who didn't want to be reasoned with.

Sometimes I'd hear her crying. Not the loud, movie kind of sobbing, but this quiet, muffled sound that somehow hurt more. Like she was trying not to let it out but couldn't stop it. Like the sadness was leaking through the cracks in her. I would hold my breath, trying to hear what was happening, trying to guess how bad it would be that night. You learn to do that as a kid—you learn the signs. The way his boots hit the floor. The sharpness in his voice. The length of silence between the yelling. You learn how to prepare for the worst without ever being told what the worst might look like.

And then there were the nights it got quiet. Those were the scariest ones. Because silence meant something had already happened. Or was about to.

I remember one night more clearly than I want to. I must've been around seven or eight. I woke up to a strange stillness. No yelling. No music. Just silence, heavy and unnatural. Something didn't feel right. I got out of bed and padded downstairs, the steps creaking under my feet. I remember that sound—it echoed in my chest like a warning. When I turned the corner into the kitchen, I saw blood on the floor. Bright against the linoleum. The back door was open—broken, actually. Hanging crooked on its hinges like someone had kicked it in. And my mom... she was on the floor.

She wasn't moving much, just moaning softly. There was a cut on her forehead, and blood was smeared down the side of her face. I froze. My body went cold. I didn't scream. I didn't even cry. I just stood there, trying to make sense of it. My little brain couldn't. It just kept looping: This isn't real. This isn't real.

I remember thinking she looked so small. My mom, who usually moved with this busy, bustling energy—always cooking or cleaning or yelling at me to pick up my toys—was suddenly so still. And the kitchen smelled like something burnt. Like something wrong. I backed up slowly and went to my room and hid. I don't even remember what happened next. The memory just... cuts off. Like my mind turned the volume down to protect me.

That was the thing about our house—it didn't protect you. The walls didn't keep the bad out. They just held it in.

Another time, I remember the dogs. We had a few, but they never lasted long. At first, I'd name them—give them personalities, little backstories in my head. I'd talk to them like they were friends. But then one would be gone. Just like that. My dad would say it ran away, or it got sick. But even at that age, I knew better. I remember the day I stopped naming them. It was after I came home from school and heard the most awful sound coming from the basement—this high-pitched scream, not human but close. My dog. My sweet, shaggy dog. I followed the noise to the top of the stairs and stopped. The door was cracked, and I could hear my dad yelling, cursing, the sound of a belt hitting flesh. The yelping got louder. Then it stopped. Just... stopped.

I couldn't go down there. I didn't want to know. But I did see something—tufts of fur on the stairs. Big, ripped-out clumps like something had been dragged. I turned and ran to my room and buried my head under my pillow. I never saw that dog again. He never came back.

I think that was the day I learned that some love just disappears.

Dinner time was another landmine. We'd all sit around the table pretending to be a normal family. My mom would make a full meal, set the table nice, try to act like everything was fine. We'd sit stiffly in our chairs, chewing quietly, waiting. Always waiting. Because it didn't take much. A look. A word. A bite taken the wrong way. My dad had these eyes—wild, darting, like he was always chasing something only he could see. You never knew what would set him off. But you knew it was coming.

One night, I remember everything was perfect—at least by our standards. My mom had made a roast, mashed potatoes, vegetables, even a chocolate cream pie. I remember how proud she looked, bustling around the kitchen, smoothing her apron, smiling like she was trying to will this dinner into peace. We were waiting for my dad to come in. I had a good feeling for once. I thought maybe we'd make it through a meal without yelling.

He came in the door, slammed it behind him, and stood in the kitchen doorway with this... look. I've never forgotten it. Like he wasn't seeing us at all. His eyes were bloodshot, his hands clenched into fists. He looked at the table, and suddenly he screamed, "Don't eat the corn!"

We froze. I was holding my fork halfway to my mouth.

My mom stood up slowly, confused. "What? What's wrong?"

He started ranting—said the food was poisoned. Said my mom was trying to kill us. His voice got louder and louder, and then he flipped the table. Just like that. Plates shattered. Glass spilled everywhere. He picked up the chocolate pie and threw it against the wall. I remember watching it slide down the wallpaper, leaving a brown smear that would never come out.

He grabbed the trash can and started shoving everything into it—the roast, the potatoes, the pie tin. All of it. My mom was crying, saying, "Please stop. Please. I worked all day on this." And he just kept going. Like he couldn't even hear her.

I didn't eat that night. None of us did.

It was moments like that that taught me how fragile peace was in that house. How quickly it could be ripped away. I learned to hold my breath,

CHAPTER ONE

to read moods, to stay small. I learned that love didn't always mean safety. And that sometimes, the people who are supposed to protect you are the ones you need protecting from.

I don't think kids should ever have to learn that.

But I did.

Before I ever learned how to multiply or tie my shoes, I learned how to disappear. How to keep secrets. How to survive.

And the house? The one with the cracked walls and bloodstains and chocolate pie on the wallpaper? That house held all of it.

It was never just a house.

It was the first place I was broken.

And for a long, long time—I thought it would be the last.

* * *

There was a time in my life when dogs felt like the only safe thing in the world. Before I even understood what it meant to be protected, or cherished, I knew how to curl up with a warm dog on the floor and pretend like everything outside that little circle of fur didn't exist. Their ears listened better than any adult ever had. Their eyes didn't carry judgment or confusion or suspicion—just quiet loyalty. I think that's why their loss cut so deeply. Because the house I grew up in wasn't just the kind of place where people broke—it was the kind of place where even the dogs didn't make it out.

When I look back, there wasn't just one dog, or even two. There were several. It felt like we always had a new one. A revolving door of wagging tails and hopeful brown eyes. And for a while, each time a new one came into the house, I got excited again. I'd give them a name. I'd sneak them scraps under the table. I'd whisper secrets into their fur when the yelling started, or when I needed to disappear for a little while. I'd tell them how scared I was. How much I wished someone would save me.

And every time, they'd listen like they understood every word.

Until one day, they wouldn't be there anymore.

Sometimes it happened quickly. One day they were at my feet during breakfast, and the next, they were gone—vanished like they'd never existed. Other times, I'd start noticing little signs. The leash still hanging by the door, untouched for days. Their food bowl left in the corner but never filled. And then the quiet would set in. The kind of silence that pressed up against your ears and made everything feel wrong. I'd ask where they were. I always asked.

And I always got the same answer: "It ran away."

That was my dad's go-to phrase. Like dogs just packed their tiny invisible suitcases in the night and slipped out the back door without saying goodbye. I wanted so badly to believe him the first few times. But even as a child, I knew better. Because dogs don't just run away in the middle of the night. Not when they've been fed, and loved, and curled up next to a kid who kisses their nose goodnight. No, they don't run away. They leave when they've been hurt. Or taken. Or worse.

The moment that truly changed me—the one that hardened something inside my chest—was the day I heard one of them scream.

It was after school. I was around nine, I think. I walked into the house like any other day, the weight of my backpack pulling at my shoulders, the same knot in my stomach I always had when I opened that door. The lights were off, which wasn't unusual. My mom wasn't in the kitchen. There was no dinner smell. Just quiet. That quiet again. The kind that made the hairs on my arms stand up.

I dropped my bag and walked toward the kitchen when I heard it. This high-pitched, gut-wrenching sound coming from the basement. It wasn't a bark. It was a scream. And underneath it, the sound of a man's voice—my dad's voice. Angry. Shouting. The crack of something hard hitting something soft. A belt, maybe. Wood. I don't know. But I heard the thud. And the whimpering. And then the screaming again.

CHAPTER ONE

I stood at the top of the stairs, frozen. I could see the first few steps going down, the darkness waiting below. And on those steps? Clumps of fur. My dog's fur. Chunks of it. Big enough that I could still see the color, still smell the dirt and warmth of him in it. I knew that fur. I had buried my face in that fur every night. I had fallen asleep crying into that dog's side more times than I could count.

I don't know how long I stood there. I just remember my legs feeling like they'd stopped working. My chest was tight, my hands shaking. I didn't scream. I didn't run. I just backed away slowly. Quietly. Like if I didn't move too fast, maybe I wouldn't be next.

That was the last time I saw that dog.

And after that, I stopped naming them.

What was the point? Why keep giving pieces of my heart to something I knew I'd lose? Why keep setting myself up to care only to have that love destroyed, one leash, one scream, one clump of fur at a time? It was easier to stop hoping. Easier to detach. Safer. At least then, when they disappeared, it wouldn't hurt as much.

But of course—it always still hurt.

You don't forget the sound of something innocent being hurt. You don't forget the silence that follows it. And you sure as hell don't forget the way the people around you pretend nothing ever happened.

Nobody in that house talked about the dogs. Not really. My mom would look away when I asked. My dad would laugh like I was stupid for caring. And me? I learned to stuff it down. Just add it to the growing pile of things I didn't know how to process: the yelling, the broken plates, the blood on the floor, and now—the disappearing dogs.

I think that was the start of me building a wall inside myself. Not out of bricks, but out of silence. Every scream I didn't answer, every question I stopped asking, every name I refused to give... it all became mortar. I thought if I could shut off the soft parts of me—the parts that loved, that felt, that needed—then maybe I'd be safe. Maybe I wouldn't feel so broken when something or someone I loved got taken away again.

But even walls have cracks. And mine started to crumble every time I'd hear a dog barking in another yard. Every time I saw a kid walking down the street, dragging a leash behind her, grinning at the pup beside her. I'd ache in a way I didn't have words for. Because I had never known what it was like to keep something. To hold love and have it stay. All I'd known was how to grieve quietly, how to pretend like the loss didn't matter, how to keep smiling even when my chest was caving in.

I remember telling myself once, "I'll have a dog of my own someday. One that no one can hurt. One that stays." And even now, decades later, that ache is still there. That longing. That quiet promise I made to the little girl version of me, standing at the top of the basement stairs, fists clenched, holding back tears.

When I got older and tried to explain some of this to people, I could see their faces change. You can talk about abuse, and people will nod. You can mention trauma, and they'll say how sorry they are. But when you talk about the dogs, something shifts. Because somehow, that part feels even more unforgivable. The loss of innocence—yours and theirs. The cruelty for no reason. It's not just violence—it's a particular kind of evil that people don't want to believe exists.

But it does. And it lived in my house.

In those early years, it felt like everything good was temporary. Anything warm or joyful or kind was something you had to hide, protect, or expect to lose. I started applying that lesson to everything. Friendships. Toys. Teachers I liked. I never let myself get too attached. I never let myself believe anything good would last. Because in my world, it never did.

And yet—some small part of me still hoped. Still looked for that wagging tail. That warm fur. That safe love. Maybe because that's what kids do. No matter how many times we're let down, we keep reaching for love. We keep trying to find it, even in the darkest places. Even when we're told, over and over again, that it's not meant for us.

I wonder sometimes if those dogs knew. If they understood, even in their short time with us, that they were loved. That at least one little girl saw them as more than something disposable. That I named them, even if no one else remembered their names. That I prayed for them. That I loved them as fiercely as a scared child could.

I hope they knew.

And I hope wherever they are—wherever they ended up—they're running free. Safe. Whole.

The pain of those memories never really left me. I've carried them like stones in my pocket. But over time, I've tried to turn them into something else. Into compassion. Into protection. Into promises. I've tried to make sure the animals in my life now are treated with tenderness. I've tried to break the cycle.

And I've learned that you can mourn things no one else understands. That grief doesn't need permission.

I still think of those dogs. Especially the one from the basement.

I still remember the sound.

And I still remember what silence followed.

* * *

There are certain things in life that are supposed to be safe. Dinner is one of them. You grow up seeing families in commercials laughing around a table, passing mashed potatoes and wiping kids' chins with napkins. On television, even the most chaotic homes still seem to pause for dinner. It's portrayed as this sacred time where food brings people together and, somehow, love is always baked into the meal.

But in my house, dinner was a minefield.

The table wasn't a place of peace or comfort. It was a stage where fear wore many faces. And no matter what was being served, it always came with a side of tension. We all knew it—my mom, my siblings, and me. We sat on edge, every fork scrape and footstep in the hallway a warning that things could flip in an instant.

I used to watch my mom try so hard. That woman could set a table with quiet grace, placing each fork like it might change the outcome of the evening. She'd hum softly while she cooked, but I always wondered if the hum was for us or for herself—a way to drown out the dread. Her hands moved quickly but carefully, chopping vegetables and flipping meat, smoothing whipped cream over a pie like it might calm the storm coming through the front door.

I remember one evening more vividly than the rest. I was probably around eight or nine. My mom had been cooking all afternoon—chicken, mashed potatoes, fresh corn, and even a chocolate cream pie. I can still smell it in my memory. The whole house smelled like hope. She wore one of her better blouses, had even curled her hair a little. She wanted it to be a good night. Maybe she had convinced herself it could be.

I think we all did.

The table was set. I was sitting at my spot, swinging my legs under the chair, nervous but hopeful. My dad hadn't come home yet, which usually meant we had a few more minutes of calm. My mom was watching the window, glancing toward the clock. She pulled the pie from the fridge and set it on the counter with a little smile. That smile made me want to believe we might just get through dinner.

And then... he walked in.

The door slammed harder than it needed to, and he was already muttering as he came in. His eyes darted around the room like he was searching for something to blame. His boots were muddy. His coat was half off his shoulder. And then he saw the food.

That should've been a good thing, right? A hot meal. A family waiting. But instead, he froze. His whole body stiffened. I could see the

CHAPTER ONE

wildness in his eyes shift into something darker. He stormed into the kitchen and stood over the counter. We all held our breath.

Then he said it: "Don't eat the corn."

That sentence didn't make sense to me at first. I thought maybe he was joking. But his voice was sharp. Accusing. My mom turned around slowly, like she already knew what was coming. "What?" she asked, gently.

"I said—don't eat the corn. Don't eat any of this. She's trying to poison us!"

He yelled it. Full volume. His voice cracked like a whip across the room. And then... he snapped.

Plates flew. The bowl of mashed potatoes crashed to the floor. He grabbed the corn dish and threw it straight into the trash, slapping it out of my mom's hands. The chocolate pie followed—smashed into the garbage like it was toxic. He shouted things I couldn't understand. Said my mom was trying to kill us. Said she had laced the food. Said she was working with someone to take him down.

It didn't matter that none of it was true. In his head, it was. And in our house, his reality was the only one that existed.

I sat there, frozen, my fork still in my hand. My mouth had gone dry. My stomach twisted into knots. I didn't know if I should run or stay still. And my mom—God bless her—she didn't cry. She didn't yell back. She just started cleaning. Silently. Sweeping up the broken plates, wiping mashed potatoes from the floor with shaking hands, while he paced and ranted and kicked the chair legs on his way back out the door.

We didn't eat that night.

And it wasn't just about the food. It was what the food represented. My mom had tried so hard to create a sliver of normal, a moment of peace. She had hoped we could have one evening where the table didn't feel like a place of punishment. But he stole it. Like he always did.

That night left a mark on me. Not just because I went to bed hungry.

But because it taught me something about how quickly joy can be taken. It was the night I learned that no matter how warm the house smells, no matter how carefully the pie is sliced, danger doesn't always knock. Sometimes it bursts through the door and throws everything in the trash.

After that, I stopped feeling excited about dinner.

I stopped hoping.

Because even when things seemed okay, we all knew how quickly they could turn. It wasn't just the outbursts. It was the unpredictability. One day, dinner was fine—quiet, even pleasant. The next, we were ducking plates and hiding in our rooms. There was no rhythm, no pattern, no way to predict it.

Sometimes, the food itself became the trigger. If the potatoes were too lumpy, the meat too dry, the corn not sweet enough—it was her fault. My mom's fault. My fault. Everyone's fault. And if the food was good? Well, that could make him angry too. Because then he'd accuse her of trying too hard. Trying to make him like her. Trying to cover up her secrets.

You couldn't win.

And I started to dread the clatter of plates. The clink of forks. The low hum of my mom's voice asking if anyone wanted seconds. Because beneath it all was the tension. That quiet, ever-present fear that any second, it could all go wrong again.

I learned to eat fast. Quietly. Without drawing attention. I'd cut my food into tiny bites and chew carefully, nodding if asked questions, always polite, always small. I tried to become invisible at the table. Not because I didn't want to be there—but because being seen meant being vulnerable.

I started associating food with fear. Not hunger. Not comfort. But fear. And even today, it's something I still wrestle with. I find myself holding my breath at the table sometimes, like I'm waiting for someone to flip. I catch myself apologizing if the toast is too dark, if the soup's too salty. It's this old reflex. Like I still think a wrong bite will bring back the rage.

It wasn't until I had my own kids that I realized just how deep that wound ran. The first time I made a big family dinner for them, I felt this pit in my stomach. I wanted it to be joyful. I wanted the kitchen to smell like butter and herbs and laughter. But as I set the table, I heard my own heartbeat in my ears. I kept checking everything—rechecking the oven, double-checking the salt, wondering if they'd hate it, if they'd snap. But they didn't. They just ate. And smiled. And said thank you.

And I cried.

Because I realized something that day: I had been waiting for something bad to happen. Even decades later, I still flinched at joy.

Dinner isn't supposed to be dangerous. But in that house, it was. And the table—meant to be a gathering place—had become a battleground.

Even now, if I walk into a room and smell gravy and mashed potatoes, I don't just think of Thanksgiving. I think of that night. That pie. The trash can full of a meal made with love and destroyed in rage.

There's a grief that lives in moments like that. Not just for the meal. But for what could've been. For the family we never got to be. For the safety that was never ours.

But I've learned something, too.

I've learned how to reclaim the table.

Not in big, dramatic ways—but in small ones. In lighting a candle. In folding napkins softly. In asking someone if they want seconds and actually meaning it. In baking bread with my own hands, letting it rise with quiet hope. In pouring love into a bowl of soup and watching someone I love go back for more.

I've learned that food can still be sacred. That meals can be healing. That even if your childhood table was shattered, you can build a new one. One where no one yells. No one throws things. No one is afraid to speak.

It's taken me years. Decades, really. But I'm finally starting to believe that dinner doesn't have to hurt. That it can be warm. And sweet. And quiet, in the best way.

And every time I set the table now, I whisper a little promise to that younger version of me—the girl who sat with clenched fists and a tight stomach, afraid to breathe.

I tell her: This is for you.

This peace is for you.

This love—safe and soft and real—it's all for you.

Chapter 2

The day he left, the house went quiet in a way I thought meant peace. At ten years old, I didn't have the words for it. I just knew that for the first time in a long time, the yelling stopped. The footsteps no longer sounded like thunder, and no one was throwing things across the room. The floor didn't shake with rage. That kind of silence, when you're a kid, feels like a miracle.

I remember coming home and seeing him packing his things into the trunk of the car. There was no goodbye, no explanation. Just a trunk that didn't want to close all the way and a man too angry—or maybe too broken—to say anything to his daughter. I just stood there watching him shove shirts and socks into bags like he was late for something. I didn't cry. I just froze. I think part of me was waiting for him to scream. Waiting for the storm. But the storm had passed, and all that was left was a strange kind of stillness.

And I thought: maybe it's over. Maybe now we can breathe.

At first, it did feel like relief. There were no more late-night fights waking me out of sleep. No more blood on the floor or broken doors. The dogs stopped disappearing. I could come downstairs in the morning without bracing myself for what I might find. It felt like the house was exhaling after holding its breath for too long. But what I didn't understand then was that silence can be loud too. It can press against your chest and make you feel just as small as the violence did. Because when the yelling stopped, something else settled in—and that was the grief.

The kind of grief no one talks about. The kind where you're relieved the chaos is gone but you miss the idea of a dad. You miss what he was *supposed* to be. You miss the imaginary version of him more than the real one. The dad I'd pictured in my head—the one who kissed scraped knees and clapped at school plays—he never existed. But I still wanted him. I still waited for him to come back and be that guy.

Instead, he was just... gone. And his absence echoed through every room like another kind of scream. I started noticing the way the house stayed dark longer in the mornings. The way my mom would sit at the table long after her coffee had gone cold. She didn't cry, not really. But she wasn't there either. Her sadness didn't come in sobs—it came in silence. In the way she stared past me. In the way her voice dropped an octave. In the way she no longer hummed while she cooked.

I think she was just trying to survive in her own way. I know that now. But back then, it felt like she'd packed herself away too—just like he did.

She got quiet. Detached. Her sadness hardened into something sharper. Something that stung when you got too close. I remember asking her a question once—just something small, something about dinner or homework—and she snapped so fast I jumped. It wasn't the answer that hurt. It was the reminder that she wasn't reachable anymore. Not in the way I needed. Not in the way a little girl needs her mom when her dad disappears.

She was doing her best. But her best looked like keeping busy and keeping numb. The dishes were always done. The laundry folded. But we weren't *talking*. We weren't connecting. We were just two people floating through the same house, trying not to look at the space he used to take up.

And the silence? It filled everything. I used to think I wanted quiet—

after all that yelling, who wouldn't? But the truth is, silence after trauma doesn't always mean peace. Sometimes it means there's no one left who knows how to talk about the pain. The TV stayed on longer. I'd turn the volume up a little more than usual. Just enough to cover the quiet. Just enough to pretend things were normal. I'd sit on the floor, watching cartoons I didn't even like, because they were *loud*. Because they didn't remind me of the empty chair at the kitchen table.

Sometimes at night, I'd lie in bed and stare at the ceiling, wondering if he was thinking about us. Wondering if he ever regretted leaving. Wondering if he even remembered my birthday was coming. He didn't call. Didn't write. Didn't show up. And I didn't ask questions about him anymore because I already knew the answers.

But I missed him. Not who he was—but the version of him I *wished* he could have been. That's the part that hurts the most when someone who's supposed to love you walks out—you don't just grieve the loss of them, you grieve the loss of who they should've been. The bedtime stories they never told. The dances they didn't show up for. The moments they were supposed to stay for—and didn't.

My mom tried to fill the gap in her own way. She started dating. It was like she needed to erase the version of life we had with him. Furniture moved around. New plates, new curtains. The way she moved through the kitchen changed. Less cooking, more takeout. Less time at home, more nights out. She was trying to move forward. But it didn't feel like we were rebuilding. It felt like we were drifting.

The worst part was how normal everyone pretended it all was. At school, no one asked. No teacher pulled me aside. No one offered a kind word. I went to class, did my work, and smiled when I was supposed to. And then I went home to a house that felt like it was falling apart in slow motion.

And I carried it all quietly.

I didn't talk about the blood on the floor or the broken door. I didn't talk about the dog in the basement. I didn't tell anyone how scared I still was when I walked through the house alone. Because who was going to believe me? Who would even know what to say?

I remember once, after school, I walked into the kitchen and saw my mom sitting at the table staring into space. She wasn't crying. She was just… gone. Her hand rested on a coffee mug, her eyes blank. I said "hi" and she didn't even hear me at first. When she finally looked up, she forced a smile, but it didn't reach her eyes. That smile haunted me for years. It was the kind of smile that says, "I'm here, but I'm not okay."

And in that moment, I realized something big: she was surviving, but she wasn't healing. Just like me.

We both learned how to live with the silence. We learned how to pretend the calm meant we were safe. But deep down, we were still walking on eggshells—only now, there was no one to scream. Just the memory of what it felt like when they did.

That's the thing about trauma—it lingers. Even when the source is gone. It leaves fingerprints on everything. On the way you brush your hair. On the way you stir your coffee. On the way you sit at the dinner table, never quite relaxing, because part of you is still waiting for something to go wrong.

And life without him? It wasn't loud. It wasn't violent. But it wasn't peaceful either. It was quiet in the most aching way. A house filled with spaces we didn't know how to fill. A home we didn't know how to call home anymore. And a mother and daughter who didn't know how to reach each other.

Not yet.

But we were trying. In our own, broken ways.

Even if all we could manage was just getting through another day.

* * *

CHAPTER 2

The quiet didn't last long after my dad left. You'd think maybe life would've calmed down—that the tension and fear would've loosened its grip once he was gone. And for a minute, maybe it did. But then the house changed again. This time, not with fists and accusations, but with noise. Loud, wild noise. And people. Men. Booze. Music that thumped through the walls long after I was supposed to be asleep.

The house that once had felt like a war zone turned into something else entirely. Not safe—but chaotic in a different way. The kind of chaos where nothing felt predictable. Where my mom traded in fear for distraction. She didn't want quiet anymore. She wanted people. She wanted to feel alive again, I think. And she didn't care what it cost us.

I was still just a kid, but I knew something was off. I'd wake up to strangers in the living room, the scent of beer and sweat clinging to the air. The floor would be sticky. Ashtrays overflowing. Sometimes I'd peek out of my room and see my mom laughing in a way I hadn't seen before—loud, slurred, tossing her hair while some guy wrapped his arm around her like they'd known each other forever. But by morning, they were usually gone. Except for the hangover—and the feeling that the house had once again stopped being a home.

Eventually, one man started hanging around more than the others. He had that look—sunglasses on even at night, reeking of cologne and liquor, like he never really left the bar. At first, he acted friendly, even playful. My mom seemed taken with him. He made her laugh, brought over bags of groceries sometimes like he was trying to impress us all.

But something about him gave me a weird feeling from the start. The way his eyes would linger too long. The way he'd sit a little too close. I didn't have words for it then, but I knew I didn't like him.

And then one night, everything shifted.

It was late. The music had died down. My mom had gone out—ran to the store for more booze, she said—and left us there, me and a friend of mine who was sleeping over. I remember the two of us giggling in my room, whispering under the covers, like little girls do. The house was dark except for the flickering hallway light, and it was finally quiet.

Until it wasn't.

He came into the room, reeking of alcohol, standing in the doorway like he belonged there. My stomach dropped. I went still. I knew something was wrong.

He came closer, sat on the edge of the bed like it was no big deal. Like this was normal. He started talking, low and slurred, asking strange questions that made no sense to me. Then his hand reached for me.

I froze.

His hand went up under my nightgown, touching me in places no one ever should. I wanted to scream. I wanted to disappear. But I just… went numb. My whole body stopped. Then he grabbed my hand and made me touch him. I still remember the sick, burning shame in my stomach. I didn't know what to do. I didn't know how to move. I was just a kid.

My friend saw and ran for my mom. But she wasn't there. She had left us. The house was empty except for me, my friend, and him.

I don't know how long he stayed in that room. All I know is when he finally left, I curled up so tight I could barely breathe. I felt like I had been stained. Ruined. Like the air itself didn't want to touch me.

The next morning, I walked out into the hallway and saw him coming out of the bathroom. He didn't say anything. Just looked at me, smug. Like nothing had happened. Like I was invisible.

I felt so ashamed. So exposed. I was a child, and already I had learned how heavy shame could be—even when it wasn't mine to carry.

But what crushed me the most… was that my mom knew. I told her. I told her what he did.

And she let him stay anyway.

For months after, he kept coming around. Sitting on the couch like he belonged. Laughing with her. Drinking. Taking up space like he hadn't shattered something inside me. I had to see him—hear his voice, smell his cologne—knowing what he'd done. And knowing that the one person who was supposed to protect me didn't send him away.

That broke something in me.

That night didn't just change how I felt about him. It changed how I saw my mom. I stopped feeling safe with her. I stopped feeling safe, period. Because if she could know what happened and still let him back in—still choose his company over my safety—then what did that say about my worth?

I was just a girl. A little girl who didn't have the words to fight back or the power to make him leave. All I had was my truth. And when that wasn't enough, I stopped telling it.

* * *

There's a kind of silence that doesn't just fill a room—it fills your body. It wraps itself around your lungs, presses into your chest, and settles somewhere deep in your stomach. It's the silence that follows something awful, something too big to talk about. And when it first moves in, it doesn't leave.

After that night, that's the silence I carried.

I didn't have the words for what had happened. I didn't even understand the full weight of it yet. But I knew something had been taken from me. Something had shifted inside me, and I didn't know how to make it go back. The house didn't feel like a house anymore. My body didn't feel like mine anymore. And my mom didn't feel like someone I could run to.

That morning, when I saw him in the hallway, calm as ever—like he hadn't just crossed a line that should never be crossed—something in me shattered. It was like he carried no shame. None. He looked me in the eyes and kept walking, while I stood there feeling hollow. He had moved on. But I was stuck. Still there in that moment. Still underneath his hand. Still scared, confused, frozen.

And then came the worst part. I told my mom.

I told her what he did.

And she didn't send him away.

She didn't scream. She didn't rage. She didn't protect me.

Instead, he stayed.

For days, then weeks, then months.

She still let him in the house. Still smiled at him. Still chose him.

That broke me more than what he did.

Because it taught me something I've spent my whole life trying to unlearn: that my pain didn't matter. That I wasn't believable. That I wasn't worth protecting.

And even though I was just a little girl, I carried that message like a stone in my pocket. Heavy. Always there. Even when I wasn't looking at it, I could feel it.

The shame settled in my skin. I didn't know how to name it, but I felt it every time I got dressed. Every time I walked into a room. Every time someone looked at me too long. I started to feel like maybe I had done something wrong. Like maybe I was dirty. Like maybe, if I had been braver, louder, stronger—it wouldn't have happened.

But none of that was true.

The shame wasn't mine. But I carried it anyway.

And the silence didn't just come from my mom. It came from me, too. I stopped talking about it. Stopped even thinking about it in full sentences. I just stuffed it down and down until it became part of me. Like a bruise that never fully healed.

And when I look back now, I see how that silence showed up in so many parts of my life.

It showed up in the way I'd flinch when someone touched me unexpectedly. In the way I never quite trusted a closed door. In the way I smiled too much around adults, trying to keep the peace. In the way I always scanned a room, even as a teenager, looking for the exits—just in case.

I carried that fear into every stage of my life.

I didn't know how to tell anyone that I'd been hurt. I didn't know how to say that I felt like my own body had betrayed me. That I didn't feel safe in my own skin. So I learned how to pretend. I learned how to fake "fine" so well that even I believed it sometimes.

But the truth was, I never really left that room. Part of me stayed right there in that bed. In that silence. In that sick feeling of being touched when I didn't want to be. Of being used and then discarded like it meant nothing.

It wasn't just about the night he touched me. It was about everything that followed. The way the world didn't stop. The way the adults in my life just kept going like nothing had changed. The way no one said, "I believe you," or "You didn't deserve that," or "You are not broken."

Instead, I felt like I had to protect everyone else from the discomfort of my pain.

And that's the thing about childhood trauma. It doesn't just hurt you in the moment—it teaches you how to minimize yourself to make other people comfortable. It teaches you how to carry shame that never belonged to you. It teaches you how to survive by being silent.

And I survived. Oh, I survived.

But at a cost.

That silence followed me into my teenage years. Into my relationships. Into the way I saw my body, the way I ate, the way I dressed. I wanted to disappear, but I also wanted someone—just one person—to really see me. To see past the fake smile and the straight A's and the helpful attitude. To see the girl underneath who was still scared, still ashamed, still waiting for someone to say, "What happened to you was not your fault."

But no one ever did.

So I buried it deeper.

I didn't trust easily. I didn't let people in. And when I started dating, I picked people who were broken in ways I understood. I let them treat me the way I had always believed I deserved to be treated—like an afterthought. Like a burden. Like I should just be grateful someone wanted me at all.

Because when your mom doesn't protect you, you grow up thinking maybe you're not worth protecting.

That belief colored everything. My worth. My choices. My ability to speak up for myself.

And over time, it morphed into something else: control.

I became obsessed with trying to control my surroundings. My space. My routine. Because if I couldn't control what happened to me as a child, maybe I could control what happened now. Maybe if I kept things clean and quiet and predictable, the pain wouldn't find me again.

But of course, life doesn't work that way.

I still made mistakes. I still got hurt. And every time something bad happened, that old shame rose back up like it had just been waiting in the wings. Whispering, "See? You still deserve this."

I wish I could say that I left all of that behind when I grew up. But healing isn't linear. Trauma doesn't follow a schedule. You can go years thinking you've moved on—only to wake up one day with that same old ache in your chest, wondering why the sound of a man's voice makes your stomach turn or why you can't relax in your own home.

Even when I had children of my own, I carried that fear. I wanted to protect them with every fiber of my being. I wanted to create the kind of home I never had. One filled with safety and softness and trust.

But sometimes, I overcompensated. I hovered. I panicked. I tried so hard to make sure they never went through what I did that I forgot how to breathe. Forgot how to rest. Forgot how to give myself grace.

And deep down, I still felt like that little girl. The one whose mom didn't believe her. The one who was left alone with the monster.

But here's what I've learned:

The shame was never mine.

The silence was never supposed to be mine to carry.

And my worth? It was never defined by who hurt me or who didn't show up when I needed them most.

I've started learning how to speak again. Not just with words—but with truth. With the kind of honesty that sits in your bones and says, "You survived. And that matters."

I'll never forget what happened in that house. I'll never forget the way my body froze. The way my friend ran for help that never came. The way the world just kept turning.

But I'll also never forget the day I realized I didn't have to carry it alone anymore.

That I could take that shame out of my pocket and set it down.

That I could tell the truth—not for them, but for me.

That I could reclaim my body. My voice. My life.

The silence may have lasted a long time.

But I'm not quiet anymore.

Chapter 3

We packed up everything and moved to Florida when I was twelve years old. And for the first time in a long time, it felt like life was turning a corner. It was all so different—new schools, new house, new man in our lives. My mom had remarried, and everything about our new setup looked... better. Shinier. Safer, even.

The sun was always warm down there, even in January. It felt like the kind of warmth you could sink into. We had a swimming pool in our backyard. A real pool. I remember standing on the edge the first time, toes curled over the tile, the water so still and clear it looked like glass. I took a deep breath and jumped in like I was diving into my new life. I wanted that splash to wash away everything. The hurt. The shame. The memories I hadn't told anyone about. Just me and the water. For a few seconds, I felt weightless.

Florida gave us beach days, endless blue skies, and long weekends at Disney. I had never experienced anything like it. The magic of walking into a theme park as a kid—it's something else entirely. The sounds, the smells, the way the air buzzed with excitement. Cotton candy, popcorn, the music of the parade echoing through the park. And for those few hours, life actually felt light. I could almost pretend we were just a normal family. A little girl in a Mickey shirt with tired legs and a full heart.

And the cars—oh, the cars. My stepdad always had these sleek, shiny

CHAPTER 3

sports cars. They were loud and fast and drew attention everywhere we went. I didn't know much about engines, but I knew the feeling of being in the passenger seat with the windows down and the wind in my face. It felt like power. It felt like freedom. Like we had somehow made it. Like I had left all the brokenness behind in Michigan.

But as beautiful as it all looked from the outside, cracks were already forming. I could feel them, even then. I just didn't know how to name them.

We weren't allowed to sit on the furniture in the living room. That was one of the first rules. The white couches were for guests. I remember thinking it was strange—why have something you can't use? But that was how it was. Certain things were off limits. We couldn't touch the stereo. Couldn't wear shoes in the house. Couldn't use certain towels, sit in certain chairs, or even breathe wrong near the pool without getting a lecture.

And discipline? It wasn't physical, but it cut deep just the same. Get a B on your report card, and you might lose the pool for the whole summer. Talk back, and you'd find yourself grounded for weeks. Not just no TV—no books, no music, no friends, no nothing. It was all or nothing in that house. One wrong move, and the world got quiet around you. You weren't hit, but you were erased.

There was a kind of emotional ice in our home. It wasn't loud and chaotic like before—it was tight-lipped and cold. My stepdad didn't yell, but his silence was its own form of punishment. His presence filled a room in a way that made you hold your breath. You always had to wonder: is he in a good mood today? Is this going to set him off? That kind of guessing game makes your nervous system go haywire. It trains you to read a man's face before he even opens his mouth.

And my mom... she was different in Florida, too. She liked the way things looked. She liked being the wife of someone with nice cars and nice things. She liked having people over for barbecues and sun bathing by the pool. I think, in her own way, she was trying to rebuild her life too. But somewhere in the middle of all the sunshine and the smiling, she forgot I was still carrying bruises she couldn't see.

I never told her what had happened back in Michigan after that first time she chose not to act. That moment stuck in my bones—when she knew what he did and let him stay anyway. It taught me how to hold secrets. And I got real good at holding them.

So I smiled when I was supposed to. I followed the rules. I tried my best to disappear into the image they were trying to build. But underneath it all, I didn't feel like I belonged. Not really.

I remember one time I laughed too loud at the dinner table. I don't even remember what I was laughing about—probably something silly from school. But the laughter bounced off the walls in a way that clearly annoyed my stepdad. He didn't say anything. He just stared at me until I stopped. That kind of silence can gut you. It's a reminder: don't take up too much space. Don't forget yourself.

So I didn't.

I kept my laughter small. My opinions quiet. My questions few.

And then came the rules.

God, the rules.

There was one about folding the towels a certain way. Another about never touching the TV. Ever. We weren't even allowed to hold the remote, let alone choose what to watch. The shows were whatever he had on, and that was that. If we didn't like it? Too bad. We sat on the floor—never on the couches, never even on the edge of them. They were too nice for us. "For company," he'd say. So we'd cross our legs on the carpet, trying to stay still, trying not to block the screen, trying not to make a sound that might get us sent to our rooms. The floor became our place. Our place to watch, to wait, to exist quietly in the background of his world.

We couldn't leave anything out—not shoes, not toys, not even a glass of water on the counter. And don't dare ask "why" too many times. That was the quickest way to lose every privilege you had.

One summer, I got grounded from the pool for not putting my shoes away properly. The whole summer. Can you imagine being a teenager in Florida, feeling the heat stick to your skin while your siblings splashed and laughed in the pool just feet away—right outside your window—while you sat alone on the floor inside, punished into silence?

I remember lying on my bed, staring at the ceiling fan, thinking: this doesn't feel like home.

The strictness wasn't about discipline. It was about control.

But here's the thing—when your life has been chaos, even harsh control can feel like safety. It gives structure. It makes sense, even when it's unfair. So I played along. I followed the rules. I figured if I could just keep everything in order, maybe I wouldn't feel so lost.

But the cracks kept growing.

I started to feel it in my body. That heavy, constant hum of anxiety. That sense that I was always being watched, even when I was alone. I didn't know what it was at the time—I just knew I couldn't rest. Couldn't relax. I was always clenching something inside me. Bracing for the next thing.

There were days the sunshine felt like a lie. Like something beautiful stretched across the surface of something ugly. People would come over and comment on how nice our house was, how lucky we were to live in such a beautiful place. And I'd smile and nod and say thank you. But inside, I wanted to scream: You don't know what it's like.

You don't know what it's like to sit on the edge of a sparkling pool, holding your breath because one wrong joke could mean two more weeks of punishment. You don't know what it's like to eat dinner in silence, the sound of silverware on plates louder than anyone's voice. You don't know what it's like to live in a house full of beautiful things and still feel like a ghost.

I was supposed to be grateful. And I was, in some ways. Florida was beautiful. We had money. I had new clothes, a new room, a new start.

But the pain I carried didn't care about palm trees or pool parties.

It followed me.

I think we all thought the move would fix something. That if we just changed our surroundings, everything else would fall into place. But trauma doesn't work like that. You can't outrun it. It comes with you. It hides in the boxes. It rides in the backseat. It whispers when you unpack.

And it whispered to me every night when the lights went out.

You're not safe.

You're not seen.

You don't matter.

I started to believe it. Not in one big moment—but slowly, over time. With every rule I followed. Every feeling I swallowed. Every truth I buried. I became smaller and smaller inside myself. Less alive. Less sure.

The mirage of Florida was beautiful. And for a while, I almost believed it was real.

But underneath the sunshine, there were shadows.

Underneath the pool, there was pressure.

Underneath the cars and the weekend getaways and the Disney tickets, there was a girl who still hadn't been heard. Who still hadn't been held. Who still didn't feel safe in her own home.

That girl was me.

And she was still waiting for someone to notice.

* * *

It happened during summer break.

There wasn't school. There wasn't structure. Just long, humid Florida

CHAPTER 3

days that stretched on forever and a neighborhood full of restless teens looking for ways to feel grown. I was fourteen. Still a kid in so many ways—still figuring out my place in the world, still dreaming about becoming a cheerleader, still sleeping with a nightlight some nights. But that summer changed everything. That summer stole something I didn't even fully understand yet.

He was nineteen. Older. Confident. The kind of boy everyone knew—especially the girls. He had that charm, that smirk, that way of moving through the neighborhood like he owned it. And I... I was young. Naive. Looking for something that felt like attention but didn't know how to tell the difference between feeling seen and being targeted.

What happened wasn't a flirtation. It wasn't mutual. It wasn't some blurred line between two teenagers. It was assault. Plain and simple. It was being used, touched, and violated in a way that shattered my sense of safety and rewired the way I saw the world.

But what came after? That might've hurt even more.

The neighborhood didn't rally around me. They didn't ask questions or listen with compassion. They turned on me. Overnight, I became the problem. The one who "asked for it." The one "making drama." I was labeled, judged, spat on—literally and figuratively. Adults whispered. Teenagers stared. I felt the walls closing in every time I stepped outside my front door.

And my brothers? They chose the crowd.

They were still going to the public school, still in the middle of the social hurricane. I guess they thought siding with the world would protect them somehow. That if they joined in on calling me names, if they mocked me like everyone else, maybe they wouldn't get dragged into the mess with me. Maybe they'd be spared.

So they turned on me, too.

I remember hearing them call me a whore, a liar. Words I didn't even fully understand yet, but that still cut like knives. Words that came from mouths that used to make me laugh. From brothers who used to build couch forts with me and ride bikes down the block. They looked at me like I was something to be ashamed of. And that shame started to seep in, even though I knew deep down it didn't belong to me.

It was the loneliest I had ever felt.

And then school started back up. But I didn't go back to public school. My mom made the decision to pull me out. Maybe it was protection, maybe it was convenience—I don't really know. What I do know is that I was shipped off to a private school across town, where nobody knew me. Nobody whispered. Nobody stared.

But nobody knew what I had survived, either.

Starting over in that private school felt like stepping into a different world. The uniforms, the quiet hallways, the new rules. I was just this quiet, nervous girl trying to fade into the background, praying no one would ask questions about where I came from.

And then, one day, cheerleading tryouts were announced.

I don't know what made me go. Maybe it was muscle memory from the life I had dreamed about before everything happened. Maybe it was a little voice inside me whispering, "Try. Just try." So I did. I showed up. I stretched. I practiced the routines. I tried out. And somehow—I made it.

Cheerleading saved a part of me that summer had tried to destroy.

It gave me something to show up for. Something that made me feel strong, powerful, important. When I cheered, I wasn't the girl who got assaulted. I wasn't the girl the neighborhood hated. I wasn't the sister my brothers ignored. I was just... me. Loud, smiling, moving in sync with a team, jumping high and landing strong. Every stomp of my shoe on that gym floor was a reminder: I'm still here.

I went to cheer camp. I learned how to fly and how to catch. I learned how to use my voice again—literally and emotionally. Ninth grade. Tenth grade. Eleventh. I was on the squad every year. And not just on it—I was good. I was dedicated. I was consistent. By my junior year, I was being considered for captain. Me. The girl everyone left behind.

I started to believe in my future again.

But that's when it happened.

That B in Algebra.

Just one letter, one grade, one little misstep—and my world came crashing down. My mom was strict. Her rules didn't budge, not even for the daughter who had clawed her way back from devastation. A B meant consequences. And in this case, it meant quitting cheerleading.

I begged. I cried. I explained how hard I'd worked, how close I was, how much it meant to me.

But it didn't matter.

I was forced to quit.

And it broke my heart in a way I didn't know was still possible.

The one thing I had built for myself, the one space that had felt like mine, the one piece of joy I had allowed myself—it was gone. Taken. Like everything else.

It felt like a punishment. Not for the grade, but for surviving. Like I wasn't allowed to have good things. Like I wasn't allowed to want too much. Like no matter how hard I worked, no matter how quiet I stayed, no matter how well I performed... it would never be enough.

And behind it all—underneath the pain, the humiliation, the quiet rage—was that same summer memory. That moment everything shifted. That boy. That house. That betrayal.

I still had flashbacks sometimes—especially on hot days when the sun hit the pavement just right. I'd hear a laugh and suddenly remember his. I'd walk past a house with the door open and feel a chill. The past was always there. Even when I tried to run. Even when I tried to cover it up with ribbons and pom-poms and fake smiles.

I remember sitting on the edge of my bed the night I found out I had to quit. I stared at my cheer bag in the corner, still zipped, still packed from the last practice. And I cried. Not just for the uniform I wouldn't get to wear again. But for all of it—for everything I had tried to build, everything I had almost healed.

It felt like being assaulted all over again. Just in a different way.

After I was forced to quit cheerleading, something inside me snapped.

It wasn't just about the pom-poms or routines. It wasn't about missing out on pep rallies or the thrill of game nights. It was about what cheerleading represented for me—structure, purpose, healing. It had been the one thing that brought my head above water after I was pulled under by the assault and everything that followed. It was the only place where I felt like I mattered, like I was good at something again.

And when that was taken away—because of a single B in algebra, no less—it didn't feel like a consequence for a bad grade. It felt like yet another way the world was reminding me: you don't get to have nice things.

So, I quit.

Not just cheerleading. I quit school altogether.

I didn't throw a tantrum. I didn't argue or beg this time. I just... shut down. Quietly, completely. Something in me gave up. I couldn't do it anymore—couldn't sit in a classroom pretending I was okay. Couldn't keep showing up in a life that kept punishing me for trying.

And so I moved out.

I was young—too young. But I felt ancient. Like I'd already lived ten lifetimes and barely survived any of them. I didn't know exactly where I was going or what I'd do once I got there. I just knew I couldn't stay. Not in that house. Not with those rules. Not with that constant ache of being seen as a problem instead of a person.

I packed what little I had. A few clothes. A small stack of books. A box of letters I'd written to nobody and never mailed. Some cassette tapes. My favorite sweatshirt—the one that still smelled like cheer camp and freedom. I didn't have a solid plan. But at that point, any place that wasn't *there* felt like a better option.

Leaving home that young isn't glamorous, no matter what people think. There were no cozy apartments with candles and throw pillows. It was survival. Sometimes sleeping on a friend's couch. Sometimes staying with someone I didn't trust all the way, but felt like I had no other option. Sometimes staring at the ceiling in a quiet, unfamiliar room and wondering what in the world I'd just done.

But you know what? In a strange, hard-to-explain way... it was also the first time in a long time I felt like I had some say in my own life.

Was I safe? Not always. Was I stable? Not even close. But I was out. I was away from the yelling, away from the judgment, away from the home that didn't feel like home.

And that meant something.

People like to ask why girls leave home young. Why they "throw their life away." But they don't often ask what pushed them out. They don't sit in the silence of what it means to lose your safe places one by one until you've got nothing left to stand on. They don't look at how trauma stacks itself like bricks on your chest until breathing under the roof you grew up in feels impossible.

I didn't leave because I wanted to rebel. I left because staying felt like dying.

It wasn't until years later that I'd even understand the language for what I was feeling back then—trauma, PTSD, survival mode, freeze response. But in that moment, I didn't need the terminology. I just knew I had to go.

The world I stepped into wasn't kind. But I had been living in unkindness for so long, it didn't feel that different.

Except this time, I wasn't pretending.

I wasn't smiling through family dinners while swallowing the shame of what had happened. I wasn't making excuses for my brothers when they spat ugly names at me just to blend in. I wasn't performing anymore.

I was just trying to make it.

There were nights I missed home—missed the way it was *supposed* to feel. There were days I longed for my mom to call and say, "Come back. Let's start over." But that call never came. And even if it had, I don't know if I would've believed it.

Because once you're cast out as the problem, it's hard to believe there's a way back in.

It was lonely, sure. But it was a loneliness I chose. And that gave it a different shape. It was quieter than the loneliness I'd felt surrounded by people who didn't believe me, didn't stand by me, didn't protect me. And at least now, my body wasn't bracing for the next blow. My heart wasn't waiting for the next betrayal.

I was just... floating. But at least I was floating on my own terms.

Eventually, I'd fall into more pain, more hardship. Life didn't soften just because I took a stand. But I think that version of me—the teenage girl who packed a bag and walked away from everything she knew—was one of the bravest people I've ever been.

She didn't wait to be rescued. She didn't wait to be believed. She didn't wait to be okay.

She just left.

And she survived.

And that's a story worth telling.

Chapter 4

There's a kind of silence that doesn't feel peaceful. It's not the soft hush of a sleepy morning or the quiet that comes after a long day. No, this kind of silence is heavier. It presses on your chest. It buzzes in your ears. It feels like the world is holding its breath and you're the only one who doesn't know why. That was the kind of silence I woke up to around 5 a.m. on that cold November morning.

I was tangled in the covers, half-asleep, the heater kicking on in the background, the bathroom fan humming from down the hall. My babies—just two at the time—were sleeping in their room. Everything should've felt normal. Safe, even. But something felt… off. Something made me open my eyes.

And that's when I saw him.

Just standing there. Right next to my bed. Close enough that I could see the glint of something in his hand. Close enough that I could hear the quiet rasp of his breathing.

He was wearing a white hockey mask. And he had a knife.

For a second, my brain refused to believe it. I mean, who expects to wake up to a masked man standing inches away from them, holding a hunting knife? I thought I was dreaming. I told myself I must be dreaming. I even closed my eyes again—just for a moment. Just long enough to hope it would all go away.

But when I opened them again… he was still there.

I don't know if I gasped or screamed or whispered, but I know I made a sound. And as soon as I did, he moved. Fast. Too fast. He was on me before I could even make sense of what was happening. One hand covered my mouth. The other pressed the knife to my neck.

"Don't scream," he whispered.

It wasn't the whisper of someone who was afraid. It wasn't panicked or angry. It was… calm. Cold. Almost like he was used to this. Like he'd done it before. And that chilled me more than anything. Because I realized then that this wasn't a robbery. This wasn't someone who had broken in to steal the TV or take my purse. He wasn't looking for things. He was looking for power.

He leaned down close to my ear, so close I could feel his breath against my skin. "Do you have any money?"

My heart was pounding so loud in my ears I could barely hear him. But I nodded. I told him, voice barely a whisper, "My wallet's in the other room."

He didn't move the knife. Didn't ease up.

"How much?"

"Seven dollars," I said. "I have a bank card too."

I said it because I thought maybe he'd take it and go. That maybe if I made it easy, he wouldn't hurt me. Maybe if he used the card, there'd be a camera. Maybe someone would catch him and this would end. Maybe there was a way out.

But he just laughed. This strange, dry little chuckle.

"No," he said. "That's okay."

That was the moment everything inside me turned to ice. Because I knew then—this wasn't about money. This wasn't about stealing. This was about control. And he had it.

He pulled me out of the bed. Told me to move. The knife stayed pressed into my back as I crawled toward the door. I didn't know where we were going. I thought maybe he wanted the wallet after all. I moved slow. Careful. Every inch was filled with silent prayers. Please let my kids stay asleep. Please just let this be a robbery. Please just let me survive.

But then... he stopped me.

"Get back on the bed," he said.

And that's when the pillow came down.

He pressed it over my face, hard. I couldn't breathe. I panicked. My arms flew up—instinct, I guess—and somehow, I managed to create the tiniest pocket of air underneath. Just enough to keep from passing out. Just enough to stay conscious. I don't know how I did it, but I thank God every day that I did.

Because what came next—I had to survive it.

He violated me.

I'm not going to describe every second. I don't want to. I don't need to. Anyone who's been through it knows that there are no words that can capture that kind of horror. And anyone who hasn't... I pray they never do.

What I will say is this: I stayed still. Completely still. Because I had to. Because my babies were sleeping just down the hall. Because I knew if I screamed, if I fought, if I did anything wrong—he might hurt them too. And I couldn't let that happen. I couldn't risk it.

Every muscle in my body screamed to run, to fight, to do something. But I kept whispering to myself, *Stay alive. Just stay alive.*

And then, I heard it.

A small voice, soft and confused, coming from the hallway.

"Mommy?"

It was my son. My little boy.

He must've woken up and realized I wasn't there. Or maybe he heard something. I don't know. But his voice cut through everything. I froze. My heart nearly stopped.

The man paused too. Leaned down again. Whispered, "Tell him to go back to bed."

My voice shook as I tried to sound calm. "Mommy's okay, baby," I called out. "I'll be there in a minute."

But my son didn't go away. He kept calling for me.

"Mommy? Mommy?"

Over and over.

I wanted to run to him. I wanted to scream, *Run!* I wanted to protect him the way a mother is supposed to. But I couldn't. I was trapped under the weight of someone who didn't care.

"Tell him to go back," the man hissed again.

I tried. "It's okay, sweetheart. Mommy's fine. I'll be right there."

But he didn't stop. And I was terrified he was going to walk into the room and see everything. That he'd be scarred forever. That he'd be the one to get hurt next.

So I said something I didn't plan. Something that just came out, desperate and shaky.

"I think... I think he's afraid of your mask."

There was a weird pause. I think it surprised him. Maybe it caught him off guard. And then, slowly, he lifted the mask and pushed it up onto his head. Just like that. Like sunglasses.

He turned slightly, just enough that I saw part of his face. Not the whole thing, but enough. His jaw. His mouth. The way his skin looked under the hallway light. I burned it into my brain. Because I couldn't scream. I couldn't move. But I could *remember*.

I held on to that. It was the only thing I had left.

That silent pleading? It's real. I begged with my eyes. Not for me—but for my kids. For him to just leave. To let me be their mother. To let me live.

And eventually... he did.

He whispered again. "If you tell anyone, I'll come back. I'll stab you and your kids. I mean it."

CHAPTER 4

Then he told me to count to one hundred before I moved. And I did. I counted, silently, under my breath, my whole body shaking. I don't even know when he got up. I just kept counting. Praying.

When I finally lifted the pillow, gasping for air, I was drenched in sweat. My arms were numb. My legs barely worked. But I got up. I walked to the kitchen.

The back door was wide open.

He was gone.

But he wasn't.

Because I would carry him with me forever.

That morning, I wasn't just a woman who had been attacked. I was a mother. A survivor. A human being trying to hold her world together with trembling hands.

And my son? He never knew. Not right then. He just climbed back into bed. I tucked him in. Kissed his forehead. Whispered, "Everything's okay."

Even though it wasn't.

Even though it wouldn't be for a long, long time.

But I survived.

And sometimes, that has to be enough.

* * *

I don't even know how I made it to one hundred.

I was counting in my head like I was reciting a spell. Something to hold the world together, something to keep the air moving in and out of my lungs. One. Two. Three. I don't think I was even breathing right. The pillow was still over my face. My hands were still clenched in fists beside me, barely holding space between the fabric and my mouth. My body was still frozen. Not because I couldn't move—but because I was too afraid to. He told me not to move. Told me to count. So I did.

I remember the number seventy-nine like it's been tattooed somewhere deep in my memory. By the time I got there, I thought I was going to pass out. My chest was burning. My arms were going numb. But I kept counting. That's what you do when you're terrified—you hold on to anything that might get you out alive. And in that moment, my lifeline was the number one hundred.

He said he would leave by then. That's what he told me. And I didn't know if I believed him. But what else could I do?

Ninety. Ninety-one. I felt my heartbeat thudding in my ears so loud it drowned out the rest of the room. I couldn't hear footsteps. Couldn't hear the door. Just that awful sound of my pulse pounding and the weight of the air pressing down through the pillow.

Ninety-eight. Ninety-nine.

One hundred.

I waited. Just for a few extra seconds. Just in case.

Then, I moved the pillow.

The first full breath that hit my lungs was like being reborn into a nightmare. Not relief. Not safety. Just air. My arms were shaking so bad I could hardly lift myself. I rolled onto my side slowly, carefully, like maybe he was still in the room and I'd scare him into finishing the job if I moved too fast.

The room was dim. Still. Empty.

But I didn't trust it.

I sat up, legs dangling off the edge of the bed. The floor felt miles away. I didn't feel real. None of it did. The sheets were still wrinkled from where my body had been trapped. My heart was still racing, refusing to calm down. My throat was raw like I'd screamed, even though I hadn't. I couldn't.

And that's when I saw it.

The back door.

It was wide open.

CHAPTER 4

The cold air hit me like a slap. Not because it was freezing outside—but because the air didn't belong. It was proof that I hadn't made any of it up. That he had been real. That he had come and gone and left that door open like some kind of cruel calling card.

I couldn't breathe again. My lungs had just started working, and suddenly they were shutting down. My vision went fuzzy, and I had to grab the wall to stay upright. My body wanted to collapse. My mind wanted to run. But I couldn't do either. Not yet.

I took one trembling step toward the door. Just to shut it. Just to make sure he wasn't still there, hiding in the dark. I reached out with my fingers and closed it slowly, quietly. My hand left a print on the glass—sweaty, shaking. And that's when a new wave of fear hit me like a freight train.

What if he was still inside?

I hadn't heard him leave. I hadn't heard a car. I hadn't seen his shadow disappear into the night. I hadn't heard a gate swing open or the crunch of gravel beneath his feet. What if he hadn't left at all?

I backed away from the door, my heart galloping inside my chest. Every creak of the trailer felt amplified. Every corner looked like it was holding something. Every shadow had a face. I couldn't breathe. Couldn't think. But I knew I had to do one thing.

I had to check on my babies.

That was the only clear thought in my mind. Nothing else mattered. I stumbled down the hallway to their room, and there they were—sleeping. Somehow. Still safe. Still breathing. My daughter was curled up with her thumb in her mouth, her hair messy around her cheeks. My son had his arm wrapped around a stuffed bear, his lips slightly parted. They looked like peace.

I dropped to my knees beside them and broke into silent sobs.

I didn't want to wake them. Didn't want to let the fear infect their sleep. But I needed to see them. Needed to know that they were untouched by the nightmare that had just unfolded in the next room. I rested a hand on each of them and whispered, "Mommy's here. Mommy's here."

And even though I felt like I was shattering into a thousand pieces—I meant it.

I was still here.

Still their mother.

Still holding it together somehow.

I don't remember walking to the kitchen. I don't remember picking up the phone. I just know that I did. I dialed the neighbor. I couldn't think of what to say. As soon as she answered, I started crying again. Talking too fast. My words jumbled, spilling out in pieces that didn't make sense.

"There was a man... in the house... he had a knife... the pillow... my kids..."

She came right over. I think she was still in her robe. Her face went white when I told her everything. And then she said the words I didn't want to hear.

"You need to call the police."

I shook my head so hard it made me dizzy.

"I can't," I whispered. "He said... he said if I told anyone, he'd come back. He'd stab me. He'd stab my kids. He said he meant it."

My whole body was trembling again. The threat still echoed in my ears like a cruel lullaby.

But she was steady.

"I'll call," she said. "You don't have to say anything. I'll make the call."

She did.

And then I waited.

I remember hearing the knock on the door and freezing again. For a split second, I thought it was him. That he had come back. That he had

CHAPTER 4

somehow known I told. But it was the police. Flashlights. Uniforms. Questions.

I stood there in my nightgown, my arms crossed over my chest, my voice barely a whisper. I don't even know what I told them. Some parts came out in a rush, other parts wouldn't leave my mouth. I could see them trying to stay neutral. Trying to gather facts. But all I felt was exposed.

I felt like I was the one under the microscope.

Not him.

I remember one officer asking, "Do you remember what he looked like?" And my mouth opened, but the words stuck. Because yes—I remembered. But I also remembered telling him I didn't see anything. That I hadn't seen his face. I had *told* him that. On purpose. So he wouldn't kill me.

What if he found out I told the truth?

What if this report got him caught—and then released?

What if he came back?

I felt like I was betraying my own survival instinct just by talking. But I did it. Somehow. I described what I could. His voice. His height. His movements. The mask. The weight of the knife. I gave them everything I had, even though it felt like I was scraping it out of my soul with a spoon.

Then they said I had to go to the hospital.

A rape kit.

An exam.

More questions.

I nodded, barely. I didn't argue. I didn't cry. I just... went.

My neighbor stayed with the kids, bless her. And I climbed into the back of a cruiser like a ghost, like someone watching herself from far away. The ride to the hospital was quiet. Nobody knew what to say. I didn't want anyone to say anything. The flashing lights from the dashboard flickered against my legs, and I stared at them like they were fireflies caught in a jar.

The hospital was sterile. Cold. Too bright.

I remember the nurse. She had kind eyes. She tried to speak gently, but I was already shut down. I laid still while they examined me, while they collected evidence, while they scraped and photographed and swabbed. I stared at the ceiling and counted again. Not to one hundred this time. Just… counting. It made me feel like I was still tethered to something.

A woman from a crisis center sat with me. I don't remember her name, but I remember her voice. She didn't push. She didn't offer false comfort. She just sat there. Steady. Quiet. And in a weird way, her presence felt like the first safe thing I'd felt in hours.

When it was all done, they gave me papers. Bags with my clothes in them. Contact info for a detective. They said someone would follow up. That I'd hear something soon.

I walked out of that hospital with the weight of the night still clinging to my skin. I felt raw. Split open. My body wasn't mine anymore—it had become evidence. My voice had become testimony. And my soul? I wasn't even sure where that was.

But I was still breathing.

That was something.

When I got back home, the sun was just beginning to rise. That pale morning light stretched across the sky like nothing had happened. The world outside looked unchanged—peaceful, even. Birds chirping. A soft breeze nudging the curtains. And me, standing on the threshold of a home that no longer felt like mine.

I walked through the front door like I was stepping into someone else's story. Everything was still and quiet, except it didn't feel calm. It felt emptied out. Hollow. My neighbor had put the kids back to bed— thank God for her—and the trailer had that early morning stillness that used to feel comforting, but now felt too quiet. Too fragile.

And then I saw the bed.

Stripped bare.

The police had taken all the sheets. The pillowcases. The blanket. All gone. Bagged up for evidence. What was left was a bare mattress, stained in places, too exposed, too raw. It hit me in the gut. Not just because of how stark it looked, but because I hadn't realized how much those things—those ordinary things like sheets and a pillow—had made the space feel like mine. Like home. Now, even that was gone.

It wasn't just the violation. It was the aftermath. The empty bed. The echoes in the hallway. The way the air felt heavier now.

I couldn't bring myself to go near it.

I walked into the hallway and grabbed the throw blanket off the back of the couch. Then I laid it on the floor, right outside my children's bedroom door, and curled up there. No pillow. No comfort. Just the scratchy texture of the carpet beneath me and the sound of my kids breathing behind the door.

And that was where I stayed.

Not because I thought I could sleep.

But because I needed to be close to them. I needed to feel like, if anything moved in the night—if anything stirred—I would be there. I could get to them in time.

I lay on that floor, staring at the ceiling, and I whispered the only words I had left in me:

"I'm still here."

And somehow, in that hollow, stripped-down moment, that was enough.

* * *

There's something about hospital lighting that makes everything feel even more unreal. It's cold and bright and far too quiet for the kind of pain you're in. That morning, I remember walking through those double doors like I was drifting in a dream I couldn't wake up from. I was escorted there—still in my nightgown, still shaking, still trying to catch my breath even hours after the nightmare had ended. But the nightmare hadn't really ended. It just shifted into a different kind of silence.

I remember sitting on the edge of the exam table, staring at the linoleum floor while someone asked me questions I didn't know how to answer. I couldn't look anyone in the eye. I didn't want to see their faces, didn't want to feel the pity or the discomfort or the judgment. And I definitely didn't want to see any softness in their eyes. Because if someone looked at me kindly, I would've crumbled right then and there. And I couldn't. Not yet.

The nurse had a gentle voice, but I couldn't absorb a word she said. She handed me a gown. She asked if I could remove my clothes. My hands moved like they belonged to someone else. Everything I did that day—every breath, every step, every word—was mechanical. I floated above myself, watching this broken woman undress behind a thin curtain, fold her nightgown, and hand it over like she was giving away the last familiar thing she had left.

They had me lie down on that paper-covered table, and I felt exposed in every way a person could feel exposed. Physically, emotionally, spiritually. There's no preparing for that kind of vulnerability, especially not when you've just lived through the worst moment of your life. They examined me gently, clinically, but all I could think about was the fact that I was being touched again. Prodded. Looked at. Measured. Photographed.

I stared up at the ceiling tiles and counted them, not because I was curious or bored—but because I needed something to anchor me. If I counted, maybe I wouldn't fall apart. Maybe I wouldn't scream. Maybe

CHAPTER 4

I wouldn't disappear completely.

That pillow never left me—not really. Even though I had ripped it off my face and thrown it across the room after he finally left, I could still feel it. The weight of it. The way it pressed down on my nose and mouth. The way I had to claw at it for air. It became a part of my skin. A part of my breath. I couldn't lie down without feeling it again. I couldn't press my head to a pillow without panicking, gasping, jerking upright like I was suffocating all over again.

Even in the hospital bed, surrounded by bright lights and people trying to help, I could feel it hovering. That invisible pillow—always just above me, just waiting to come back down.

At one point, someone from the local crisis center came in. She sat beside me, quiet and patient. She didn't ask questions. She didn't try to fix anything. She just... sat. I didn't even know her name, but I still remember her face—soft and still and full of permission. Permission to not speak. Permission to fall apart if I needed to. And even though I didn't break in that moment, I felt something shift inside me. Like my body, so tightly locked down, took one cautious breath. Just one.

But the numbness came next. It was heavy and quiet and all-encompassing. I thought I'd cry more. I thought I'd scream, throw something, break down like you see in the movies. But I didn't. I went completely still. Like someone had flipped a switch inside me and the lights went out. I smiled when I was supposed to. I nodded when someone said, "You're so brave." I answered the detectives' questions, gave them details, signed forms.

But none of it felt real.

I was floating outside myself, watching this woman give an account of what happened to her body. Listening to her describe what she saw, what she felt, what she feared. And I hated her. I hated that woman. Because she let it happen. She didn't fight harder. She didn't scream louder. She didn't protect her children better.

And that woman, of course… was me.

The numbness wasn't a feeling—it was the absence of all feeling. I didn't cry when I left the hospital. I didn't cry when I picked up my kids or walked into the shelter or laid down in a strange bed that night. I just moved. Like a wind-up toy going through the motions. I bathed my babies. I tucked them in. I kissed their foreheads like everything was okay. But inside, I was gone. Hollow. Empty.

I didn't sleep that night. Or the next. Every time I closed my eyes, I saw his face. Or rather, the mask. The way it stared blankly at me. I heard his voice in my ear—calm, cold, controlled. I felt the pressure of the knife. The weight of him on top of me. I heard my son calling for me from the hallway. And I remembered how I told him to go back to bed, even though every cell in my body wanted to scream for him to run.

My body wasn't mine anymore. Not in the way it used to be. It didn't feel like home. It felt like a crime scene. Something had happened there. Something violent. Something unspeakable. And no amount of washing, dressing, or pretending could make that go away.

I didn't want to be touched. Not even by my own children. When my daughter reached for me, I hugged her back, but a part of me recoiled. When my son climbed into my lap, I forced myself to stay still, to be present—but inside, I was pulling away. Not because I didn't love them. But because my body didn't feel like a safe place for anyone anymore. Not even for me.

The worst part was pretending. Pretending to be okay for them. Pretending to be okay for the neighbors, the police, the women at the shelter. Pretending I was holding it together when really, I was unraveling at the seams. I smiled when people said, "You're so strong." I said thank you when someone brought over dinner. I joked about being tired when I forgot something. But I wasn't tired. I was traumatized.

And no one really saw that.

Because trauma doesn't always look like panic attacks or sobbing on the floor. Sometimes it looks like brushing your teeth while staring into space. Sometimes it looks like folding laundry on autopilot. Sometimes it looks like cooking dinner while your hands are shaking and your heart is pounding and you can't even taste the food you're making.

Sometimes trauma is invisible. But it lives in your bones. In your breath. In the way you flinch when someone walks too close. In the way you scan every room before you enter it. In the way you lock the door three times and still don't feel safe.

I didn't recognize myself anymore. Not just physically, though that changed too. I stopped caring what I looked like. I stopped putting on makeup. Stopped dressing cute. I just wanted to disappear. I wanted to be invisible. If I could vanish into the background, maybe no one would notice me. Maybe I could avoid being hurt again. Maybe I could be safe.

But of course, the pain doesn't stop just because you go quiet.

The pain had moved in permanently. Not the sharp, screaming pain of the night it happened. That kind is loud and terrifying, and somehow, a little easier to name. But this pain... this was dull and constant. Like a weight I carried in my chest every single day. It wasn't always at the forefront, but it never really left either. I could be laughing at something my kids said—one of those belly laughs that comes from nowhere—and just like that, it would return. Heavy. Lingering. Like a bruise pressed too soon.

Some nights, I'd lie on the floor of my room—not the bed, I couldn't do the bed yet—and I'd trace the cracks in the ceiling with my eyes, wondering if I'd ever feel at home in my own skin again. It wasn't just about what he did to me. It was about everything I lost because of it. I lost the right to feel safe. I lost sleep. I lost the lightness in my smile. I lost the version of me who used to believe that the worst thing could never happen inside her own home.

And worst of all, I lost trust in my body. It had always been mine. Mine to dress up or rest or hug my babies with. But now, it felt like it had betrayed me. Or maybe like I had betrayed it—by not protecting it enough. That kind of thinking was dangerous, I know that now. But back then, it wrapped around me like a second skin. The shame wasn't mine, but it still stuck to me like tar.

I would scrub in the shower until my skin burned. Hot water. Harsh soap. A desperate need to feel clean again, even though I knew deep down it wasn't on the surface. It was deeper. Underneath. Buried in places no soap could reach. Still, I tried. I'd scrub and scrub, and then sink down to the floor of the tub, water pouring over me like a baptism I didn't feel worthy of. I'd sit there until it turned cold. Until I couldn't pretend the heat was helping anymore.

And I remember—I started dressing differently too. Bigger clothes. Darker colors. Anything to cover myself. I wanted to disappear. Blend in. Shrink. Be unnoticeable. Because in my head, I thought maybe if no one looked at me, I'd be safe. Maybe if I became invisible, no one would hurt me again. And for a long time, that was the goal: to vanish.

I was afraid of mirrors. Not just because of what I looked like—but because of what I didn't see anymore. There used to be a spark in my eyes, a sense of play, a softness. But that girl had been replaced by someone else. Someone who flinched at sudden sounds and hated the way her nightgown brushed her legs. Someone who couldn't lie still without hearing phantom footsteps in the hallway.

The world saw me as a survivor. And I was. I am. But back then, that word didn't bring me any comfort. It felt like pressure. Like I had to prove something. Like I had to "get better" fast, or people would stop understanding. Like healing had a deadline, and I was running behind.

But healing doesn't work like that.

Some days, I could make dinner. Other days, I couldn't get off the floor. Some nights, I could hum lullabies to my babies. Other nights, I sat with my hand over my heart, whispering, "You're okay, you're okay, you're okay," like a broken prayer. Some days, I laughed without feeling guilty. Other days, I couldn't even smile.

And all of that... was still healing.

I didn't know it then, but every breath I took after that night was a kind of resistance. Every dish I washed. Every bedtime story I told. Every moment I showed up for my kids when I didn't even know how to show up for myself. That was healing. Quiet. Unseen. But holy in its own way.

There was a day—months later—when I went to the store. Just a quick trip. Just milk and bread. But it felt monumental. I remember walking down the cereal aisle and suddenly locking eyes with a man who looked vaguely familiar. Nothing threatening about him. Just a stranger who happened to glance my way. But the panic that shot through me was instant. My heart raced. My vision blurred. I had to grip the edge of the cart to stay upright.

That was the day I realized my body had turned into an alarm system. Always ready. Always scanning. Always screaming *danger* even when none was there. It didn't matter if I was safe. My body didn't believe it. Not yet.

And so, I started listening to it.

I started letting myself sleep on the floor without shame. I started wearing what made me feel secure, even if it wasn't stylish. I started saying "no" to things that felt like too much. I stopped apologizing for needing time. And slowly—painfully slowly—I started to feel a little less like a ghost and a little more like a person.

There was no big breakthrough. No one day where the sun came out and I felt healed. It came in tiny, fragile ways. The first time I hummed while doing the dishes. The first time I danced with my daughter in the living room. The first time I didn't check the locks more than once. The first time I laughed without feeling guilty afterward.

My body still isn't fully mine. There are moments—certain positions, certain smells, certain shadows—that steal it back for a second. But I'm learning how to take it back. Not all at once. Not perfectly. But gently. Patiently.

Because my body isn't a crime scene.

It's the place that held my children. It's the arms that rocked them to sleep. It's the voice that comforted them when they were scared. It's the hands that have cooked thousands of meals, folded thousands of little socks, wiped away tears and painted pictures and braided hair.

My body is mine. Even on the days it doesn't feel like it.

Even on the days I still flinch or freeze or wake up in a sweat.

Even on the days I can't smile.

It's mine. And I'm learning how to live in it again.

That pillow? The one that once silenced me? It doesn't own me anymore. Not completely. It lives in memory, yes. In flashbacks and panic. But not in my bed. Not in my breath. Not in my present. It doesn't get to decide how I love my children, how I show up in the world, how I claim my space.

I'm still healing. Still learning. Still finding softness in a body that was once made of stone.

But I'm here.

I survived.

And I'm not disappearing anymore.

Chapter 5

When I met him, I was already in the middle of a storm—divorcing, raising three babies on my own, and trying to survive the fallout of a life I had thought was going to be different. My kids were 4, 2½, and just 7 months old. I was exhausted in every possible way—physically, emotionally, spiritually. I was vulnerable. And I was looking for something that felt like peace. Something that felt like safety. And that's what he pretended to be at first. Safe.

He was charming when he wanted to be. Attentive in a way I hadn't experienced in so long. He'd say things like, "You deserve better," and I wanted to believe him. I needed to. I was fragile. Holding my life together with bobby pins and prayer. And he stepped in like he was going to help me carry the load. I didn't see the red flags—not then. I saw someone who called me beautiful when I hadn't brushed my hair in days. I saw someone who said, "Let me help," when I was juggling bottles and laundry baskets and toddlers pulling on my clothes.

And so I let him in.

Within three months, I was pregnant again.

That pregnancy hit different. Not because of the baby—my babies were always miracles to me, always wanted, always loved—but because of what was happening around me. The shift in him. It didn't happen all at once, but slowly, in pieces. Little things at first. Possessiveness disguised as "caring." Questions that felt more like accusations. "Why did it take so long at the store?" "Who were you on the phone with?" "Why did you put on makeup today?"

At first, I answered gently. Explained. Tried to reassure him. Tried to prove that I was loyal, that I was good, that he had nothing to worry about.

But no answer was ever good enough.

Soon, he was timing me. From the moment I left to the moment I returned. The phone had to stay within his earshot. Grocery trips had to be fast—and heaven help me if I forgot something and had to go back. I was accused of everything under the sun. Cheating. Lying. Hiding things. All while I was growing a life inside me. All while I was still feeding babies, still nursing wounds from a marriage that had already left me bruised and breathless.

It was like being caught in a riptide. You don't realize how far you're being pulled out until you're drowning.

And then came the violence.

He never hit me in the face. Not where people could see. But he didn't have to. There were other ways to hurt. Bruises on my arms. My back. My thighs. Pushes that sent me into walls. Yells so loud they made my bones rattle. Slamming doors that made the babies scream. Threats whispered in my ear while I was holding a bottle or folding laundry. Control disguised as care. "I just worry about you." "I'm the only one who'll ever love you." "No one else would want you, not with all those kids."

The gaslighting was constant. The fear lived in my throat. Every day was a guessing game—what mood would he be in? Would today be calm, or would I be tiptoeing across landmines? And the worst part was—I was so ashamed. I felt like I had failed all over again. Like I had brought another monster into our lives. And I didn't know how to leave.

There was nowhere to go.

CHAPTER 5

I had no money. No family willing to help. No support. I had three small children and another growing inside me, and I was trapped.

I started walking on eggshells so finely that I forgot what it was like to relax. I'd sit at the kitchen table, fork halfway to my mouth, and freeze if the door creaked open too hard. I memorized the creaks in the floor so I'd know where to step and where to avoid. I knew how to keep the kids quiet. How to keep the TV low. How to move through the house like a shadow. My only goal: don't set him off.

But you can't stop a bomb from going off by holding your breath.

I remember one night in particular. I was seven months pregnant, my belly so big it felt like I was carrying the whole world. The kids had just gone to bed. The house was still. He came in pacing—always the sign. Something had triggered him. I don't even know what. A look I gave. A tone in my voice. Maybe I had just breathed wrong. And then, like flipping a switch, the calm was gone.

He started screaming. Accusations flew. I stood there, shaking, trying not to cry, because crying made him angrier. Then he reached for the gun.

I still hear that sound in my nightmares.

He pointed it at my head. Pulled the trigger.

Click.

Unloaded. Just a sick joke. A show of power.

Then he pointed it at my swollen belly. At my unborn baby.

Click.

Just that sound. That terrifying, empty click. Followed by a grin that chilled me to my core.

"I could," he said. "Just remember that."

That night, I curled around my belly and sobbed silently. I was too scared to cry out loud. I didn't want to wake the kids. I didn't want them to see their mother broken. Again.

I knew then: I had to get out.

But how?

* * *

There's no way to really describe what it feels like when someone puts a gun to your head and pulls the trigger.

The sound it makes—that sharp, echoing *click*—it doesn't just ring in your ears. It roots itself into your bones. And the terrifying part is that for a second, just a split second, you don't know it's empty. Your body doesn't wait for the truth. It panics. It mourns. It prepares for death. Every time.

He did it once and stared at me, eyes locked on mine.

Click.

Then he did it again.

Click.

And again.

Click.

Four times in total. Each click felt like my life was being gambled away, like I was in some twisted game he was playing by himself. Russian roulette, except I was never allowed to say no. I was just the target. The actress, as he liked to call me when I cried.

And then he beat me.

He didn't just hit me—he unleashed everything. I remember falling, my knees hitting the floor. My hands over my head. The way his fists came down. The way he grabbed my hair so hard it felt like my scalp was being peeled away from my skull.

And when it was over, when I finally managed to pull myself up from the floor, there was so much hair scattered around me it looked like someone had brushed out a shedding dog. Just globs. Tufts. Strands everywhere. It felt like pieces of me were left behind in that mess. And still... I stayed.

CHAPTER 5

I stayed because I didn't know how to leave.

Because I was pregnant, because I had babies in the other room, because he timed my grocery runs and tracked every step I took. Because I wasn't just scared—I was trapped. And I didn't know where to go that he wouldn't find me.

Until that night. The night he said it.

"Tonight I'm going to kill you."

He didn't whisper it. He didn't yell. It came out flat, like a weather report. Just a fact. Like, *tonight there's a 90% chance of your death.* My crying started immediately, because I believed him. I fully, completely believed him.

And when he called my mother, put her on speakerphone and told her what he planned to do—*that they'd be picking me up in a body bag*—I felt something inside me break. Not just fear. It was like watching a door lock behind you. Because she didn't stop him. She didn't scream or plead or call the police. She just... listened. And I realized, *I'm on my own. No one's coming. No one's going to stop this.*

But I would.

Somehow, I would.

That night, I stayed awake while he slept. I laid there with my eyes open, hand on my belly, feeling the tiny kicks of the life inside me. I kept thinking, *You can't grow up here. I won't let this be your story too.* My other babies were asleep down the hall. I pictured their faces. I thought of the way they looked at me with trust. I thought of the gun. I thought of the *clicks.*

And I made the decision: *We are leaving. Tonight.*

* * *

I didn't have a plan. Not really. I had fear and a few seconds of quiet while he was snoring in that bed like nothing ever happened. I remember sitting up slowly, trying not to make the mattress creak. My whole body ached—from the beatings, from the pregnancy, from the sheer weight of terror. But I moved.

I crept down the hall and peeked in on the kids. They were asleep. My babies. My everything. My son was wrapped up in his favorite blanket, the one with the rockets on it. My toddler had her hand up by her cheek, thumb tucked between her fingers like she always did. My baby was sucking his thumb and sleeping soundly. And in that moment, I knew. *They're not going to grow up in this. I will not let them.*

I didn't take anything. No clothes, no diapers, no pictures. Just them. I remember standing there frozen for a second, looking at my purse like, *Do I have time to grab it?* And then I thought—*what if he wakes up while I'm digging through it?* So I didn't. I just slipped on shoes, picked up my babies and walked out the front door into the night.

The door didn't even slam shut. It clicked behind me, like it was letting me go.

The air hit me like a slap—cold, still, real. I didn't have a car. I had no idea where I was even going to go. But I didn't turn back. I walked.

My arms burned from the weight of the kids, but adrenaline is funny like that. It makes you superhuman when you need to be. I walked blocks, barefoot on the inside of my shoes, belly cramping, heart pounding. I was watching every corner, every streetlight, praying to God he didn't wake up and come looking.

Eventually, I found a payphone outside a gas station. I fished around in the change cup—it was a miracle there were coins in there—and I called the only number I could think of: the women's shelter. I had remembered seeing a flyer in the bathroom at the grocery store once. I had memorized the number "just in case." And thank God I had. The woman on the other end picked up, and I didn't even say hello. I just said, "I have three kids. I'm pregnant. He has a gun and said he's going to kill me. Please help me."

CHAPTER 5

She did.

She told me where to wait. I hung up the phone and sat on the cold concrete. I wrapped my arms around my babies and waited. Every car that passed made me flinch. Every set of headlights felt like it could be him.

But eventually, a van pulled up. A woman stepped out—plain clothes, kind face, calm voice—and said, "Are you Jana?" I nodded, too exhausted to even speak. She opened the back door, helped me buckle the kids in, and then she helped me into the front.

I cried the entire way.

Not because I was scared anymore—but because for the first time in so long, I wasn't.

The shelter wasn't what I expected. I don't know what I thought it would be, maybe cold or hospital-like. But it was warm. There were other moms there. Other kids. Other people who had stories written in bruises and whispered prayers. It didn't feel like a home, not at first—but it felt like safety. And that was more than I had in years.

The first night, I barely slept. Not because I was scared—but because I wasn't used to the quiet. Real quiet. No shouting. No footsteps pacing the hall. No threats. No locks clicking behind me. Just the distant sound of traffic and the breathing of my babies in a bed beside me.

They gave us a toothbrush. A comb. Diapers. Juice boxes. A clean shirt. The simplest things felt like luxuries. Like someone was saying, *You matter. You made it.*

The next few days were a blur. I met with advocates. Told my story over and over. Each time it felt like ripping a bandage off. But each time, I also felt a little bit stronger. A little more like *me*. They helped me file a restraining order. Helped me apply for assistance. Helped me figure out what life might look like next.

But healing doesn't happen overnight.

I still jumped at loud noises. I still flinched when someone touched my shoulder. I still couldn't bring myself to look at my reflection without seeing what he'd taken. But I was *trying*. And trying is beautiful in those early stages.

My kids started to laugh again. That's what got me the most. My toddler giggled over applesauce. My son chased a ball in the backyard of the shelter. I sat on the porch steps and cried—not out of sadness, but because I hadn't heard their real laughter in so long.

It wasn't easy, of course. Starting over never is. I had nothing but my kids and a deep, bone-tired determination to give them a life better than what we'd come from. I was still pregnant. Still worn out. Still afraid. But I was free.

And freedom is worth every sacrifice.

I remember one afternoon, maybe a week after arriving at the shelter, folding donated clothes on the twin bed they gave us. The window was cracked open, and the breeze blew in with the scent of someone's fabric softener from the laundry room. It smelled like peace. Like "you're safe now." And I just sat there holding a little onesie in my hands, belly round with the baby I was still carrying, and thought, *We made it. We really made it.*

That man never found us. He called my mom again after I left, still threatening, still claiming I had overreacted. But I was done believing I was crazy. I knew what he had done. I knew what he had said. And even if no one else believed me—I believed myself.

I had the marks. The fear. The *clicks* of that empty gun, forever echoing in my memory.

But I also had my babies. I had breath in my lungs. I had hope in my hands, even if it trembled.

People think escaping means the end of the story. But really, it's just the beginning. That night—walking out, barefoot, swollen with pregnancy and shaking with fear—I didn't know what came next. I didn't know if I'd find a job, a home, or even myself again.

CHAPTER 5

But I knew this:
I was never going back.

Chapter 6

It didn't happen in some dramatic scene like you'd see in a movie. There was no moment where I was dramatically breaking down in a therapist's office, no sudden realization where all the puzzle pieces clicked into place. It was slower than that. Heavier. Years of buildup. Years of being told I was "too sensitive" or "too negative," or that I needed to "just try harder" to be happy. And eventually, I guess I believed it. That it was my fault. That something was just… wrong with me. That I was broken in a way that couldn't be named, couldn't be treated, just carried.

But then one day, sitting in a dull gray chair in a windowless room, someone gave it a name.

PTSD.

Severe depressive disorder.

Paranoid schizophrenia.

Three words. Just like that. Spoken calmly, clinically, like it was a routine chart update. But for me, they landed like a quiet explosion. I felt a strange mix of relief and terror—because finally, *finally*, I had names for what I'd been feeling all this time. But those names? They were scary. They felt like labels that would stick to my skin forever.

I remember sitting there, clutching a folded tissue that I hadn't actually used, and nodding like I understood what those words really meant. But I didn't. Not then. All I knew was that something inside me

CHAPTER 6

cracked open when the doctor said "Post-Traumatic Stress Disorder" out loud.

I had heard of PTSD before. Soldiers. Combat. War. That's what I thought of. Not women like me. Not moms who were just trying to make it from one day to the next. I didn't realize that trauma could live in the everyday. That you could develop it from growing up in chaos, from being touched when you shouldn't have been, from hearing your own son's voice calling out for you while you lay under a pillow fighting for air. That trauma didn't need a battlefield. Sometimes it grew up in your childhood home.

Suddenly, memories I had buried under blankets of numbness started floating to the surface. The constant scanning of rooms. The jumpiness. The way my heart pounded at harmless sounds. The way I couldn't sleep in a bed or go to the store without my hands sweating. It wasn't just me being "nervous" or "on edge." It was my brain trying to protect me, long after the danger had passed.

And the depression—God, the depression was like this thick fog that had followed me since I was a little girl. I could fake a smile. I could function. I could make dinner and braid hair and fold laundry and nod along with the best of them. But inside? It was like walking through a world where all the colors were dulled. Where laughter echoed but didn't stick. Where everything, even the good things, felt like they were being filtered through glass. The diagnosis of severe depressive disorder didn't surprise me as much as the others. It felt like a name for a guest that had been living in my house for years, eating at my table and sleeping in my bed.

But the third one... that one hit different.

Paranoid schizophrenia.

That one was a punch to the gut.

I remember staring at the word on the paper like it wasn't even English. I kept rereading it, like if I blinked enough, it would change. I felt something inside me shrink. That word came with so much baggage. So many images I didn't want to be associated with. That word felt like something you whispered behind closed doors. Not something you said out loud in the middle of a Tuesday.

And yet... it fit. It explained things I hadn't wanted to admit even to myself. The voices. The shadows in the corners of rooms that weren't really there. The overwhelming sense that someone was watching me. Listening. That something bad was just around the corner, always. I hadn't told anyone how bad it had gotten. I had kept it inside because I didn't want to be seen as "crazy." I already felt like people looked at me like I was fragile—like I might fall apart if the wind blew too hard. What would they say if they knew I sometimes heard voices that weren't mine?

But hearing the diagnosis, as hard as it was, also gave me a strange kind of freedom.

It gave me *permission*.

Permission to stop pretending everything was okay.

Permission to seek help without feeling ashamed.

Permission to look at my life, and all the hell I'd been through, and finally say, "No wonder."

No wonder I couldn't sleep.

No wonder I panicked in grocery stores.

No wonder I jumped at shadows and triple-checked the locks and flinched when someone touched my shoulder.

No wonder I felt like I was drowning even in calm waters.

I wasn't crazy. I wasn't weak. I wasn't just "dramatic." I was injured. Wounded in a way that no one could see. And finally, someone had named it.

The road after that diagnosis wasn't easy. It didn't magically make everything better. If anything, it made things harder for a while. Suddenly, I was being handed medications and therapy referrals and

CHAPTER 6

brochures with titles like *Living with Schizophrenia*—as if those glossy pamphlets could sum up the nightmare of waking up at 3 a.m. to voices that didn't belong in your mind. I had to try different meds, some that made me feel like a zombie, others that made me gain weight, lose sleep, lose pieces of myself.

I remember standing in the mirror one day, over 300 pounds, my face puffy and tired, my eyes hollow. I didn't recognize myself. The medication was saving my mind but burying my body. And even when I started to lose weight—over 100 pounds—I couldn't bring myself to keep going. Because as miserable as I was in my skin, I was also *safe*. I didn't want the attention. I didn't want eyes on me. I didn't want to be looked at, noticed, admired. Because the last time I was those things... I was hurt.

The weight became armor.

Heavy, suffocating armor—but armor all the same.

So I stayed in that in-between space. Half-healing. Half-hiding. Desperately wanting to feel better, but terrified of what "better" might bring. It's a strange kind of grief, grieving the person you might have been if trauma hadn't set up camp in your life. If the fear hadn't taken root so deep that even freedom felt dangerous.

Therapy helped, slowly. Not right away. At first, I hated every second of it. I hated digging into the past. I hated talking about things I'd spent years trying to forget. But over time, I started to understand the importance of giving voice to the things that had hurt me. Of not letting shame grow in silence. I talked about my childhood. The dogs. The blood. The screaming. The nights I pretended to be asleep so I wouldn't get noticed. I talked about the assault. The intruder. The violence. The way it all lived in my muscles, in my jaw, in the way I folded towels like I was trying to keep something together.

And the voices—yes, even the voices—I talked about them too. Slowly. Carefully. Like I was handing someone a piece of glass. I explained that they weren't loud, not always, but they were convincing. That sometimes they sounded like people I knew. That sometimes they told me I wasn't safe. That people were talking about me. That the world wasn't real.

The therapist didn't flinch. She didn't shrink back. She didn't label me with fear.

She just nodded and said, "That sounds exhausting."

And it *was*.

It still is, some days.

But that's the thing about naming something—it doesn't make it disappear, but it gives you something to fight. Something to work with. Something to understand.

Before, I was fighting shadows.

Now, I knew what I was up against.

PTSD.

Severe depression.

Paranoid schizophrenia.

They sound clinical on paper. But in real life, they show up as exhaustion that feels bone-deep. They show up as dishes left in the sink for three days because you can't find the will to care. As locked doors and drawn curtains. As smiles that don't reach your eyes. As isolation. As fear. As survival.

But they also taught me something.

They taught me what resilience looks like.

It's not always pretty. It's not always inspiring. Sometimes, resilience looks like brushing your teeth when everything in you wants to go back to bed. Sometimes it's making tea. Sometimes it's just staying alive another day.

And even now, decades after the worst moments of my life, I'm still learning what healing looks like. Sometimes, healing means taking your medication even when you hate the side effects. Sometimes it means forgiving yourself for the days you couldn't get up. Sometimes it means letting someone in, even when your brain tells you not to trust them.

Sometimes healing looks like writing your story.

And naming every monster out loud.

Because once something has a name, it has less power.

It doesn't disappear, but it shrinks just enough for you to stand a little taller. To breathe a little deeper. To whisper to yourself, "I made it through."

And that, for me, is where healing really begins.

* * *

For a long time, I was a prisoner in my own home. Not in the obvious way—with bars or chains—but in the quiet, haunting way that no one really talks about. I didn't go outside unless someone took me. I didn't walk into the sunlight just to feel it on my face. I didn't roam the aisles of the store like a woman with errands to run. I stayed inside. I paced. I watched the windows. I checked the locks. I lived life behind a curtain of fear. The world outside didn't feel safe. But the world inside my head? That was worse.

Sometimes my mind pulls me back to places I don't want to go. Not to relive them. Not because I choose to. But because trauma doesn't ask permission.

It doesn't knock gently and wait to be invited in. It doesn't whisper softly and ask, "Is now a good time?" No, it creeps in. It catches me off guard in the quietest, most tender moments—when I'm stirring soup, or folding towels, or humming to the rhythm of dishwater. It slips in under the music. It floats through the hum of the fridge. And suddenly,

I'm not in my kitchen anymore.

I'm back there again.

Not clearly. Not like a movie with a beginning and end. Just fragments. Blurry, disjointed, emotionally charged pieces of a story I never asked to live. My mind tries to protect me, and in doing so, it's wiped away pages I'll never get back. But some images are too heavy, too jagged, too etched into my soul to ever disappear.

There's one I can never forget. One that still makes my breath catch in my throat.

I was lying in a hospital bed.

I don't remember which hospital. I don't know what year. The faces blur together. The buildings all looked the same—gray, sterile, humming with fluorescent lights and institutional coldness. But I remember how I felt: terrified, confused, and completely alone.

I was naked.

The door was wide open.

People walked by—staff, patients, maybe both—and they looked in. Not one of them looked away. They looked right through me like I wasn't even there. Like my body on that bed wasn't a body. Like I wasn't a person, just another broken thing lying on a sheet.

I remember trying to pull the covers up. Just something. Just one tiny piece of fabric to shield my soul. I wasn't even thinking about modesty—I was begging for dignity. I wanted to feel human. I wanted to feel *safe*. But every time I reached up and pulled the covers over myself, they yanked them back down.

Over and over again.

And then someone barked at me.

A woman—someone who worked there—looked at me like I was being difficult, like I was being dramatic, and snapped, *"They're all women here!"* As if that was supposed to make it better. As if women can't humiliate each other. As if that stripped the shame off my skin and gave

CHAPTER 6

me back my peace.

It didn't.

I laid there exposed. Physically. Emotionally. Spiritually.

And I remember whispering inside my head, *I don't understand what I did wrong.*

I wasn't violent. I wasn't lashing out. I wasn't yelling or fighting. I was scared. I was lost. I was trying to make sense of why I couldn't sleep, why I kept hearing voices, why the walls seemed to breathe and close in around me. I was there to get help.

But in places like that, you don't have to do anything wrong to be punished.

You just have to exist.

And for them, that was enough.

I wish I could say that was the only time something like that happened. But it wasn't.

It happened more than once. Different hospitals. Different staff. Same feeling.

Other moments sneak up on me. They hit in waves. Sometimes soft. Sometimes brutal. But always without warning.

Strip searches.

Yes. Strip searches. When I was brought into the psych unit. In front of cameras. In front of strangers. No curtain. No privacy. No respect.

I stood there, humiliated, bare in every way a person can be bare.

I looked around the room, searching for just one face that looked human, just one person who might say, *This isn't okay.* But no one said it. No one looked away. No one reached out.

They had me stand. Turn. Bend. Lift.

And then... nothing.

No comfort. No kindness. Just a crumpled set of thin paper pants and a scratchy top that didn't even fit—ripped every time I moved. They tossed it at me like I was a number. Not a name. Not a story. Not a mother. Not a woman who had survived more than anyone in that room could imagine. I wasn't a person.

I was a "case."

That's what it feels like when your diagnosis swallows your identity. You're no longer *Jana*. You're the bipolar woman. The schizophrenic. The paranoid patient. The one with trauma. The one with scars too deep for charts to explain.

I lost something in those rooms.

Not just my freedom. Not just my memories.

I lost my dignity.

I lost my ability to believe I was worthy of kindness. Of softness. Of safety.

And maybe the cruelest part?

I don't even have all the memories to process it. Just shards. Fragments. Flashes of cold air, cold stares, hands too rough, voices too sharp.

I carry it.

Not always on the surface.

Most days, you wouldn't see it in me. You'd see the woman wiping down the counter, humming to herself in the kitchen. You'd see me folding towels or baking biscuits or lighting candles before dinner. You'd see calm.

But underneath? There's grief.

Not just sadness. Not just anger.

Grief.

For the girl I was before all of this. For the version of me who still believed hospitals were places of healing. For the woman who thought mental illness didn't mean losing your humanity.

And that grief? It doesn't go away.

It rides with me. Quietly. Steadily. Through homemaking. Through faith. Through every act of reclaiming who I am.

CHAPTER 6

I still flinch when a door slams too hard.

I still panic if someone walks into a room too fast.

I still check the locks twice. Three times.

I still keep a flashlight by my bed—not because I'm afraid of the dark, but because I remember what it felt like to be in a room with no control.

And yet... I'm learning something.

Even now. Even after all these years.

I'm learning that it's okay to be angry.

I'm learning that I'm allowed to grieve.

I'm learning that just because I survived, that doesn't mean what happened to me was *ever* okay.

Because it wasn't.

And it wasn't my fault.

And even if no one ever says they're sorry—

Even if I never get a letter, or an apology, or a single acknowledgement from the people who hurt me—

I can still speak the truth.

My truth.

I can say, *That was not okay.*

I can say, *I deserved better.*

I can say, *You didn't get to take my voice.*

Because that's the thing about trauma—it doesn't just live in your memories.

It lives in your skin. Your spine. Your nervous system. It breathes through your blood and curls itself around your heartbeat.

Even if the mind forgets, the body remembers.

But now?

Now I remember too.

I remember who I am *outside* of all that.

I'm a mother. A homemaker. A painter. A baker. A woman with a voice that's quiet but firm. A woman who lights candles at night not just for ambiance, but because she knows what it's like to live without warmth.

And I've chosen to live again.

To love again.

To speak again.

To tell my story—not just the parts that hurt, but the parts that heal.

Because somewhere in those hospital rooms, under the layers of trauma and confusion, under the diagnoses and the shame...

I never stopped being me.

I was just buried.

But not anymore.

* * *

I didn't really know what it meant at first—*the diagnosis.* PTSD. Severe depressive disorder. Bipolar. Paranoid schizophrenia. The words didn't land all at once. They sort of floated in the air around me like confetti after a parade no one asked for. I wasn't shocked. But I also wasn't sure what to do with it. It felt more like a label than a lifeline. Something stamped across my life like *damaged goods.* Something doctors would use to explain away the pain I hadn't even fully unpacked myself.

By the time they stuck me in the locked unit, I was already unraveling. But nothing prepares you for what that really means—those white walls, the stiff, scratchy sheets, the metal toilets, the long hallways where the lights always hum but no one ever really sleeps. I remember the way the doors shut behind me. That cold, sterile sound. Not like closing a door at home. It sounded more final. Like I was being locked out of the world.

And maybe I was.

CHAPTER 6

The first few days blurred together. Time didn't feel real there. It stretched and dragged like wet laundry. I couldn't tell if it was morning or night unless someone came in and shoved a paper tray of food at me. Even then, I'd just stare at it. Most of the time I didn't eat. Couldn't. My appetite wasn't just gone—it had been buried beneath layers of confusion, fog, and meds that made my head spin and my hands twitch.

They said I was a danger to myself. I didn't argue. Not because I agreed—but because I didn't have the energy to disagree. I didn't care. That was scarier than any diagnosis, honestly. I just... didn't care anymore. I didn't care what happened to me. I didn't care about the meds or the rules or the fact that I hadn't felt like myself in years. I didn't even feel like a *self* anymore. Just a floating, heavy presence they kept trying to sedate.

And they did. Oh, they did.

They forced injections on me when I refused to take the pills. Held me down, stuck the needle in, and let the drugs flood my system until I couldn't tell where the pain ended and the fog began. I'd sit in that plastic chair in the corner of the group room, staring at nothing, feeling like a ghost. Everyone around me had their own shadows—but we weren't allowed to talk about them. Not really. Not openly. Just forced "check-ins" and color-coded charts and blank stares from nurses who looked tired in their eyes.

After one particularly strong injection, I lost the ability to feed myself. My hand wouldn't cooperate. I'd try to lift the fork to my mouth and it would veer off to the side, jabbing my cheek or pressing into my nose like I was some kind of puppet with cut strings. It was humiliating. It was terrifying. And it was *real*. That wasn't something I'd read about in a pamphlet or seen in a movie. That was my body betraying me—because of a shot I didn't want, didn't ask for, and couldn't stop.

When I was released, I wasn't better. I was worse. Numb in a way that didn't feel protective anymore. Numb in a way that felt permanent. I shuffled out of there like a zombie. I don't even remember what the discharge instructions were. I just know I was supposed to "follow up" and "take my meds as prescribed" and "report any changes." As if I had the presence of mind to report anything when I couldn't even sit up straight on my own.

My daughter fed me when I got home. That's how far gone I was. I couldn't eat on my own. She held the spoon to my lips like I was a child again. Like I had reversed time and fallen back into needing someone else to help me do the most basic thing a person needs to survive. And the whole time, I wanted to scream. Not because I was in pain, but because I was *still here.* Still breathing, somehow, in a body that didn't feel like mine. In a brain I didn't recognize anymore.

I forgot how to laugh.

That might sound small, but it broke me in a way nothing else did. I'd see something funny—a joke, a commercial, my kid doing something silly—and the response wouldn't come. I'd know it was supposed to be funny. I could even remember what it used to feel like to laugh. But the laugh itself was gone. Trapped behind a wall I couldn't find the door to.

And it wasn't just the laugh. It was all of it. The spark. The little bits of joy that used to peek through the cracks. A hot shower. A favorite blanket. A warm cookie. They didn't feel like anything anymore. I went through the motions. Sat on the couch. Folded laundry. Took my pills. Pretended. But inside? It was just... blank.

People called it recovery. But what was I recovering? A broken version of myself I barely remembered? A life that had never really felt safe to begin with? The truth is—I wasn't recovering. I was *enduring.*

I was still seeing shadows where there weren't any. Still checking locks, even though I knew the locks wouldn't save me. Still panicking if the power flickered or the house creaked at night. Still hearing whispers that weren't there. And yet somehow, I was expected to function. Expected to show up to appointments and fill out paperwork and answer questions like I was capable of answering anything honestly without it being used against me.

The meds made me gain weight. A lot of it. Over 100 pounds. It was like watching your body morph into someone else's in slow motion. I could see it happening, and I couldn't stop it. Couldn't *care* enough to stop it. Couldn't move my body the way I used to. Couldn't summon the motivation to try. And in some sick way, I felt safer that way. I didn't *want* attention. I didn't want eyes on me. I didn't want to be looked at, noticed, admired, approached. I wanted to disappear.

The weight felt like protection. Like a layer of armor. Like a barrier between me and anyone who might try to hurt me again. And yes, I hated how I looked. Hated how it felt to move. Hated the way the world treated me because of my size. But the fear of *not* having it—of going back to being small and visible and *vulnerable*—was stronger than my desire to feel good in my own skin.

And so I stayed there. Trapped in a loop of fear, meds, survival, silence.

I stopped trusting my brain.

Stopped trusting doctors.

Stopped trusting myself.

But somewhere, in the quiet that followed the storm, I realized I wasn't dead.

I was still here.

And if I was still here... maybe that meant something.

Maybe it meant I wasn't done yet.

Maybe it meant there was still a reason.

I didn't jump into recovery like some big, beautiful breakthrough. I tiptoed into it. Crawled, some days. Sat still in it. Let it come to me, little by little. There were days when just brushing my teeth felt like a victory. Days when smiling at my reflection, even for a second, felt like a step forward.

And there were setbacks. Big ones. Days when I hated myself all over again. Days when I cried for hours and couldn't remember why. Days when I thought I'd never feel normal, never be able to laugh, never be able to live a day without fear scratching at the back of my mind like claws on a door.

But there were glimmers too.

Moments when I held a warm cup of tea and felt it soothe something in me.

Moments when I saw the sun hit the kitchen window just right and felt a flicker of peace.

Moments when my daughter wrapped her arms around me—not to feed me, but just to hold me—and I realized I was still worthy of love.

Learning to live with it isn't about erasing what happened.

It's not about pretending the white walls didn't break me or that the shots didn't steal something from me.

It's about saying: *Even with all that, I am still here.*

It's about picking up the pieces one by one, even when they cut your fingers.

It's about finding the sacred in survival.

And it's about letting yourself believe—however slowly, however cautiously—that healing is still possible.

Even when the world goes on without you.

Even when you forget how to laugh.

Even when your body doesn't feel like your own.

Even when the mirror reflects someone you barely recognize.

You are still here.

Chapter 7

There was a time in my life where the scale said over 300 pounds, and somehow, that still felt like the least of my heaviness.

I didn't get there overnight. It didn't come from one decision, or even ten. It came from years of trying to numb the ache, of swallowing pain with food because it was the only thing I could control. Because when everything else felt so out of reach—peace, love, safety, sleep—a cookie didn't ask me questions. A second helping of dinner didn't judge me. Late-night snacks kept me company when the house got too quiet and the thoughts got too loud.

It started when the depression hit hard—really hard. The kind that made my bones feel heavy before I even got out of bed. The kind that made everything feel pointless. Washing dishes, brushing my hair, answering the phone... it all felt like too much. Some days I didn't shower. Some days I wore the same clothes three days in a row. Some days I laid on the couch and stared at the ceiling for hours.

That was around the time I started the medications. I had finally been diagnosed—PTSD, severe depression, bipolar disorder, and later, paranoid schizophrenia. It felt like someone had finally put a name to all the chaos in my head, but there wasn't any comfort in it. Just more appointments. More pills. More side effects. And a brand-new kind of exhaustion that no nap could touch.

The meds helped keep me alive. I'll never deny that. But they also made me feel like a stranger in my own skin. They slowed everything down—my thoughts, my energy, my emotions—and made me feel like I was walking through wet cement. And they made me hungry. Not regular hungry. Not "let's have dinner" hungry. But ravenous, aching, insatiable. Like there was a black hole in my stomach that food couldn't fill but I kept trying anyway. Eating made me feel something. Or at least, it made me feel less. And in those days, feeling less was the closest thing to relief I had.

I'd tell myself it was just a snack. Just a treat. Just a little something to get me through. But then it would turn into a second helping, a late-night binge, a secret trip to the kitchen while everyone else was asleep. I'd eat standing at the stove. I'd eat while hiding wrappers in the trash so no one would see. I wasn't eating because I was hungry. I was eating because I was lonely. Because I was tired. Because I felt like a failure and didn't know what else to do with that feeling. Because food was the only thing I could rely on to not leave.

And the more I ate, the more I hated myself for it. I could feel the shame growing just as fast as my waistline. I'd catch my reflection in a window and turn away before I had to really look. I stopped buying mirrors. Stopped going to stores with harsh lighting. Stopped letting myself be in photos. I didn't want to see myself because the person I saw didn't feel like me. She felt like someone who had given up. Someone unrecognizable. Someone no one would love.

I'd stand in front of the mirror and pick apart every inch of myself. The way my stomach hung, the way my arms jiggled, the way my thighs rubbed raw. I'd wrap myself in oversized clothes, not to be comfortable, but to disappear. To hide. To protect myself from being seen.

Because somewhere deep down, I was terrified of being seen again.

Being invisible had started to feel like safety. I had spent so many years being watched by the wrong kind of eyes—judged, abused, violated—that now, any attention at all felt threatening. Compliments

CHAPTER 7

made my skin crawl. Eye contact felt dangerous. The idea of being attractive again brought up a kind of fear I couldn't explain, only feel. I told myself, "If I'm big, I'll be safe." If I'm big, no one will look at me. If I'm big, I won't be desired. If I'm big, I won't be hurt.

I convinced myself that the extra weight was protection. Armor. A shield. That if I just stayed this way, no one could get close enough to break me again. But that armor became a prison too. Because while I was hiding from danger, I was also hiding from life. From joy. From connection. From myself.

And still, I kept eating. Even when it hurt. Even when I hated myself afterward. Even when I cried after dinner because I swore I'd eat better today but didn't. I would sit on the edge of my bed, out of breath from walking up the hallway, knees aching, face flushed, and think, *How did I get here?* And the answer was always the same: I survived. That's how.

The food, the meds, the weight—they were all part of how I survived.

They were part of how I kept going in a life that kept knocking me down. Part of how I filled the hours when grief got too loud and loneliness got too heavy. They were part of how I made it through nights where sleep wouldn't come and mornings when the sun felt cruel.

But even though I understood *why* it happened, that didn't make it any easier to live in the aftermath. The shame was constant. I felt like I had failed not just myself, but everyone. My kids. My partner. The younger version of me who once had dreams and hope and a waist small enough to wrap her hands around.

There were times I avoided doctors just so I wouldn't have to step on the scale. Times I skipped family events because I didn't want to be the biggest one in the room. Times I cried while trying to squeeze into pants that had fit just a month ago. I would stand in dressing rooms, sweating, humiliated, and leave without buying anything. It felt like the world wasn't built for people like me. Like I didn't belong in it anymore.

And yet—despite all of it—I still longed to feel beautiful again. To feel strong. To walk into a room without shame riding shotgun. To wake up and not feel like I was dragging the weight of my body, and my past, and my guilt behind me.

I knew the weight wasn't just physical. It was emotional. It was historical. It was ancestral. It was every time someone told me I wasn't enough, every time someone touched me without my consent, every time I was abandoned or betrayed or belittled. I had carried it all, and now I was carrying it visibly. My trauma wasn't just in my heart anymore. It was on my hips. On my arms. On my belly. And I hated that anyone could see it.

But healing doesn't happen overnight. And it doesn't always look like progress. Sometimes, healing is standing in front of the mirror, tears in your eyes, and saying, "You're still worthy." Sometimes it's eating a real meal instead of skipping dinner to punish yourself. Sometimes it's going for a walk, not to burn calories, but just to feel your lungs work.

There came a point when I realized I had to forgive myself for the way I survived. I had to stop punishing myself for the choices I made in the darkest chapters of my life. I didn't choose trauma. I didn't choose to live in fear. I didn't choose to be hurt. But I did choose to stay alive. And for that, I deserved compassion.

So I started learning how to offer myself grace. Slowly. Painfully. Imperfectly. I started journaling. I started praying again. I started cooking with intention, not just to eat, but to nourish. I started lighting candles in the kitchen and playing soft music while I cleaned. I found therapy in stirring batter, in organizing spices, in folding laundry.

The weight didn't fall off all at once. And it wasn't linear. I'd lose some, gain some, lose more, then plateau for months. But I kept going—not because I hated my body, but because I wanted to feel at home in it again.

And I lost over 100 pounds.

CHAPTER 7

That in itself was a miracle. A hard-won, sweat-soaked, tear-stained miracle.

But here's the truth that not everyone understands: losing weight didn't magically erase the fear. In some ways, it brought it back. As I got smaller, I noticed people looking at me differently. Complimenting me. Smiling at me longer. And that old panic would rise in my chest like smoke. *They see me now. I'm visible again.*

And that terrified me.

Because deep down, there was still a voice whispering, *If they see you, they can hurt you. If they want you, they can break you. If you're beautiful again, you'll be a target again.*

I found myself self-sabotaging. Eating late at night when I wasn't hungry. Skipping walks. Making excuses. Gaining a little back. Holding myself at a weight that still felt hidden. Safe. Invisible.

It's a strange kind of prison—wanting so badly to be free of the weight, but fearing what that freedom might bring. Wishing I could shed the pounds like I shed the shame—but knowing they were tied together like roots under the surface.

Even now, I wrestle with it. With wanting to be healthy but not wanting to be seen. With knowing I deserve to feel good in my body, but fearing what attention might come with that.

But every day, I try again. I light the candle. I drink the tea. I look at myself in the mirror—not to criticize, but to see the woman who survived. The one who kept showing up for her children, for her healing, for her life. The one who bore the weight of trauma, of grief, of 300 pounds—and still found a way to rise.

And that, to me, is strength.

Real strength.

Not in what the scale says.

But in what I say to myself now.

I am still here. And that matters more than any number ever will.

***

It wasn't some big, dramatic moment when I decided to change. There was no music swelling, no lightning bolt of motivation. It was quiet. Subtle. One of those moments where you look at yourself in the mirror and feel the ache—not just in your knees or your back, but in your spirit. The kind of ache that says, "Something has to give." And for me, it had to be the weight. Not just the weight on my body, but the emotional load I'd been dragging around for years.

I started slowly. Secretly. I didn't make announcements or post before-and-after pictures. I didn't even tell anyone at first. I wasn't looking for applause—I was honestly afraid of what attention might come if people started to notice. The extra weight had always been a kind of armor. It made me invisible in a world that had hurt me too many times. And part of me wanted to stay that way. Hidden. Safe.

But another part of me... it whispered that maybe I could do this. Maybe I could take control of something. So I did it quietly. No gym memberships. No diet fads. Just small, stubborn choices that felt almost insignificant in the beginning. More water. Less sugar. More movement. Less numbing out.

I remember walking in my tiny living room at first—just pacing back and forth while something baked in the oven. It wasn't glamorous. I didn't have workout clothes or a Fitbit or any of the "right" tools. I had old sneakers, a cheap scale, and an internal war that never seemed to end. Every pound I lost felt like a fight. A whisper of rebellion against the lies I'd been told—that I was stuck. That I was broken. That I couldn't do hard things.

But I did. Quietly. Day after day.

Nobody really saw the work I was putting in. Nobody clapped when I passed the fifty-pound mark. Nobody threw confetti when I dropped under 250 for the first time in what felt like forever. There were no celebrations, no parties. Just me, standing alone in the bathroom, staring down at the scale, both proud and scared out of my mind.

Scared because every pound gone meant I was becoming more visible. And that visibility... it brought up something dark. A fear I didn't even realize I was still carrying. I didn't want to be looked at. I didn't want to be noticed. That kind of attention never brought anything good into my life. So I lived in this strange space—caught between wanting to be healthier, to feel better in my body, and wanting to stay hidden so I'd never be seen the way I was seen before.

Every milestone I reached came with a mixture of pride and grief. I'd stand in my closet, trying on clothes I hadn't worn in years—clothes that used to pinch at my arms or pull too tight at the waist—and I'd feel this strange numbness. I should've been excited. But most of the time, I just felt... alone.

I wanted someone to say, "I see how hard you're trying." But the truth was, I didn't even fully let people in. I didn't want the attention. I didn't want the compliments. Because deep down, I still believed that being noticed was dangerous.

I remember the first time someone said, "You look great, have you lost weight?" and my stomach flipped. Not in a happy way. In a panic way. It felt like a spotlight had suddenly been turned on. I smiled politely. Said thank you. But inside, all I could think was: I want to disappear again.

Because even though the physical weight was coming off, the emotional weight was still heavy. The memories. The fear. The way trauma settles into your skin and convinces you that your body is a liability. That if you make it smaller, you're vulnerable. That if you become attractive again, the danger returns.

That's the thing people don't always understand about weight loss after trauma. It's not just about discipline and willpower. It's about safety. It's about trust. It's about confronting the layers of protection we've built around ourselves and choosing—sometimes trembling—to let them fall.

There were nights I'd cry in the shower after weighing in. Not because I was disappointed, but because I was terrified of succeeding. What would happen if I kept going? Would it bring the past back? Would it invite attention I couldn't handle? Would it make me a target again?

I kept going anyway.

One day at a time. One pound at a time.

Nobody talks about the loneliness of it. How many meals I ate with a knot in my stomach, not because I was hungry, but because I was anxious. How many birthdays passed without a slice of cake because I was too afraid one bite would lead to the spiral. How many mornings I got up early to walk in circles around my kitchen because it was the only place I felt safe enough to move my body.

I didn't take pictures. I didn't journal. I didn't want to document the process. Because what if I failed? What if I gained it all back? What if this was just another phase of trying to fix what had always felt so broken?

But I didn't fail.

I kept going.

And one day, I stood on that scale and realized I had lost over 100 pounds.

That number hit me like a wave. A mixture of shock and disbelief and pride. I sat on the edge of my bathtub and just stared at the floor. A hundred pounds. A whole person. Gone.

But even in that moment, there wasn't a celebration. There was just silence. And a question that echoed in my mind: *Why do I still feel so heavy?*

Because the truth was, even though the number had changed, I was still carrying things. The memories. The fear. The shame. The grief. The loneliness.

CHAPTER 7

But I had also gained something: proof that I was capable. That I could do hard things. That I could commit to myself and show up, even on the days I didn't want to. Even on the days I felt like a ghost in my own life.

People think weight loss is about willpower, but for me, it was about reclaiming pieces of myself. It was about finding strength in places I didn't know existed. It was about learning that I could show up for me—not for a goal, not for a size, not for praise—but for healing.

I didn't shout it from the rooftops. I didn't post transformation pictures. But I held that 100-pound loss close to my chest like a medal no one else could see.

And even though I haven't finished the journey— even though I've hovered in that space of wanting to keep going but also wanting to stay hidden—I still count that loss as one of my greatest wins.

Because I did it quietly.

I did it scared.

I did it alone.

I did it with tears in my eyes and fear in my chest.

But I did it.

And even though I'm still working on what comes next—even though I sometimes still feel torn between healing and hiding—I know this: every pound I lost wasn't just weight. It was fear. It was shame. It was pieces of the past I finally laid down.

And for the first time in a long time, I could look in the mirror—not with joy, maybe not even with pride—but with a kind of softness. A whisper in my heart that said: *You're still here. You're still fighting. You are worth the care you give yourself.*

Even if no one else claps.

Even if no one else notices.

This fight was mine.

And I was winning. Quietly. Steadily. Day by day.

* * *

There's this strange thing no one really tells you about trauma—how it can make you afraid of being seen. Not just emotionally. Physically. Seen in the most literal sense of the word. I didn't realize it right away. It crept up over the years. Subtle, but powerful. Like a shadow following me wherever I went.

At first, the weight came from depression. From medication. From survival mode. I didn't care what I ate or when. I didn't move my body because it hurt in more ways than one. I was just trying to get through the day. Trying to quiet the noise in my head. And food, well—it helped. It numbed. It distracted. It gave me tiny comforts when everything else felt too big or too broken to face.

But over time, the weight started to feel like more than a side effect. It started to feel like protection.

When I was heavier, people looked past me. Doors weren't held open. Strangers didn't strike up conversations. Men didn't stare too long. I could go through the store, pick up my groceries, and not feel like I was being hunted. That probably sounds dramatic to some people. But when you've been prey before, you never stop scanning for danger. You never stop wondering if the way someone looks at you is harmless—or the beginning of something that'll haunt you for years.

So I stayed hidden. Not just emotionally. But physically. The weight wasn't just pounds. It was armor. It was distance. It was a buffer between me and the world. And in that heaviness, I felt a twisted sense of control. I told myself: If I stay like this, I'll be safe.

I knew I wasn't healthy. I felt it in my joints, in my breathing, in the way I avoided mirrors. But the idea of getting smaller terrified me. I'd been smaller before. And I knew what came with it. The attention. The comments. The looks. And all I could think was: I can't survive that again. I can't go back to being visible.

CHAPTER 7

Even now, after losing more than 100 pounds, I find myself self-sabotaging. There are days when I feel the scale creeping down and something in me panics. I'll overeat. Not because I'm hungry—but because I'm scared. It's like my body remembers, *This is where it wasn't safe. This is where the bad things started.* And it pulls me back, trying to keep me wrapped up in this shell I built to survive.

The truth is, misery became a place I understood. It became a kind of safety.

I didn't like how I felt in my body. I didn't like the way clothes fit, or how my knees ached when I stood too long. I didn't like the way I avoided cameras or turned down invitations because I didn't want anyone to see me. But at the same time—I didn't like the idea of not feeling this way either. Because what if feeling better meant feeling exposed?

So I sat in the in-between. Miserable, but afraid to move. Unhappy with how I looked, but terrified of the version of me that might come back if I looked different. I told myself stories: If I get smaller, I'll be a target again. If I lose too much weight, people will notice. If I'm noticed, I won't be safe. I believed those stories so deeply, they became part of my identity.

And maybe the worst part of all this was knowing how irrational some of it sounded—and still not being able to shake it. Because trauma doesn't care about logic. It doesn't care about statistics or encouragement or well-meaning advice. It lives in your bones. It speaks in your own voice, in the quiet moments, whispering: *You remember what happened last time. Don't forget. Don't let your guard down.*

And I didn't.

I kept the weight. Not all of it, but enough. Enough to feel tucked away. Enough to not draw attention. Enough to keep my smile small and my presence quieter. I didn't want compliments. I didn't want curious eyes. I didn't want anyone asking how I did it—because I wouldn't know what to say. "Oh, I lost the weight through fear and control and years of self-loathing"? Not exactly something you frame on your wall.

I used to imagine what it would be like to feel completely free in my body. To wake up, stretch, and not be aware of every fold, every ache, every layer. To put on a dress and feel beautiful, not braced for a comment or a glance that would make me flinch. But I've never known that kind of freedom. Not really. And the truth is, it's hard to long for something you've never felt safe having.

So instead, I learned how to blend. How to disappear in a crowd. How to laugh just enough to be likable, but not loud enough to draw attention. How to keep my eyes down in public. How to pick clothes that didn't hug too tight or show too much. I told myself, *This is fine. I'm safe here.* And for a while, I believed it.

But deep down, I knew I wasn't fine. I was just surviving in slow motion.

There's a loneliness in this kind of fear. A shame, too. Because you watch other people change their lives and celebrate their progress and stand in the light—and you wonder why you can't do the same. Why even the thought of joy feels dangerous. Why you can't let yourself be happy in your skin, even for a moment.

I've cried more than once over a salad. Not because I don't like vegetables—but because eating healthy means taking a step toward change. And change is terrifying. It opens doors I worked so hard to nail shut. It invites things in. Eyes. Opinions. Conversations. And I wasn't sure I was ready.

Even now, on the good days—when I move my body and feel strong, when I choose water over soda or stretch a little deeper in the morning— there's a part of me that waits for the fear to crash back in. And sometimes it does. Sometimes it tells me I've gone too far. That I should back off. That it's safer in the shadows.

But I'm learning. Slowly. Gently.

CHAPTER 7

I'm learning that I don't have to punish myself to protect myself. That visibility doesn't have to mean vulnerability. That my body is not an open invitation—it's mine. And I can decide how to live in it. That losing weight doesn't mean I'm asking to be hurt again. That health isn't vanity. It's survival, too. It's a way to reclaim my space in the world, not as prey—but as a woman who has lived through hell and still rises.

Some days I still eat to numb. Some days I still avoid mirrors. Some days I still wear baggy clothes on purpose. But I'm working on it. I'm trying to sit with the discomfort instead of hiding from it. To tell myself a new story: *You're allowed to be seen. You're allowed to take up space. You're allowed to feel good in your skin. And none of that means you're not safe.*

I don't know if I'll ever be fully comfortable in my body. I don't know if I'll ever reach the number on the scale that feels "right." But maybe that's not the point anymore. Maybe the real victory is that I'm still trying. That I haven't given up. That I'm learning how to live in a body that's been through so much, and still give it grace.

Because this weight I've carried it was never just about food or fat or fitness. It was about fear. It was about shame. It was about silence.

And now, I'm finding the courage to set some of it down.

Not all at once. Not perfectly. But piece by piece. Step by step. Breath by breath.

Because I may still be scared.

But I'm not hiding anymore.

Chapter 8

It didn't happen all at once, the way people in movies talk about it. There wasn't a single defining moment where I stood up taller or looked in the mirror and thought, *there I am*. No music swelling in the background. No grand transformation. Just small moments. Subtle shifts. Quiet returns.

I remember one morning—I couldn't even tell you what day it was. I had made coffee, still half-asleep, and walked into the bathroom to splash some water on my face. When I looked up into the mirror, I expected the usual: the woman who never really looked back. But for whatever reason, that morning... I paused.

I really looked.

And she looked back.

Her eyes were tired, sure. There were creases that hadn't been there years ago, and a heaviness in the way her shoulders sat. But there was something else too. Something almost like recognition. Like underneath everything—the weight, the years, the fear—I could still see her.

Me.

It startled me, honestly. Like spotting an old friend in a crowd. You don't realize how much you've missed someone until you see them again. And then, suddenly, it's all you can think about.

For a long time, I'd been someone I didn't know. Or maybe someone

CHAPTER 8

I didn't want to know. The version of me that survived everything—she was strong, yes, but she was also disconnected. She floated. She endured. But she didn't live.

I'd look at photos of myself from years ago and wonder where that girl went—the one who would dance around the kitchen while baking a pie, or sit out on the porch watching fireflies just because it made her heart feel lighter. That girl felt like a ghost. A memory I couldn't fully grasp.

But Tim... Tim never looked at me like I was broken.

He didn't look at me like someone who needed fixing, or like he was trying to dig through the rubble to find the woman I used to be. He just looked at me—right where I was. And somehow, in his eyes, I never felt like too much or not enough. Just... worthy. As is.

He had this quiet way of loving me that didn't ask for anything in return. No conditions. No expectations. Just presence. He'd hand me my coffee in the morning with this sleepy little grin and say, "Good morning, sweetheart," and I swear there were days that tiny moment kept me from crumbling.

And the way he'd sit beside me when I didn't have the words? That mattered more than anything. He didn't try to fill the silence with solutions. He just sat. Sometimes with a hand resting on mine. Sometimes with the soft sound of a record playing in the background. Sometimes with nothing but stillness.

He never pushed me to "get better." Never made me feel guilty when I had a hard day. He made space for me. And in doing that, he unknowingly gave me permission to start making space for myself.

One night, after the dishes were done and the house had gone quiet, I walked into the bedroom and caught my reflection in the mirror again. I was in an oversized T-shirt, my hair in a messy bun. Nothing glamorous. But something in me softened.

And I whispered to my reflection—maybe for the first time in a decade—"You're still here."

I didn't cry. I didn't smile. I just stood there, letting the moment be what it was. A recognition. A tiny step forward.

The truth is, I had spent so much time avoiding myself. I didn't want to see the weight. The scars. The lines etched by worry and grief and panic. I didn't want to be reminded of everything I had lost—or everything I had survived.

But survival has a way of shaping you. It may bury parts of you for a while, but it also strengthens the pieces that remain. It builds something deeper, quieter, harder to shake. And I was starting to see that woman in the mirror—not the girl I used to be, but the woman who stayed. The woman who didn't give up.

The thing that hit me hardest, though, wasn't just seeing myself again—it was realizing how long I had been gone. How many years I'd spent going through the motions, doing everything for everyone else, trying to hold the world together, all while feeling like a shell.

It's easy to lose yourself when survival becomes your full-time job.

And yet, somehow, here I was. Still standing.

Tim would sometimes say little things—like "I love the way you hum when you cook," or "You have the most beautiful laugh"—and I'd look at him like he was talking about someone else. But slowly, slowly, those little seeds started taking root. I started believing him. Just a little. Just enough.

One afternoon, I was folding laundry and he came in, leaned on the doorframe, and said, "You're glowing today." I laughed. I told him he was ridiculous.

But later that night, after I washed my face and climbed into bed, I thought about it again. *Glowing? Me?*

And for the first time in years, I didn't immediately dismiss the compliment. I just let it sit. Let it be true—even if just for that day.

Coming back to yourself isn't a straight line. There are days you

CHAPTER 8

feel strong and sure, and then days where brushing your hair feels like climbing a mountain. But the beautiful thing is—once you start seeing yourself again, it gets a little harder to keep disappearing.

And with Tim by my side, that journey felt less lonely.

He didn't lead me back to myself. He just walked beside me while I found my way. He didn't cheer too loudly or stand with a flashlight—he simply held out his hand and stayed. That kind of love? It's rare. It's sacred.

It helped me believe I was still in there. That there was more than trauma. More than fear. More than just surviving.

That I could come back.

That I already was.

* * *

There's a kind of wanting that slips in softly, like a whisper you almost miss—especially after you've spent most of your life just trying to survive. Not the kind of wanting that burns hot or crashes in all at once, but a gentler kind. Quieter. A kind that tiptoes around the grief, careful not to wake it.

That was the kind of wanting that came back to me first.

After years of carrying trauma, raising kids mostly alone, escaping violence, navigating mental illness, and learning how to breathe again—I didn't even know how to want anything for myself anymore. My life had become a rhythm of bracing and getting through. That was what I knew. So when I started to want again, even in the smallest ways, it was startling.

It wasn't some big declaration. It started with the smell of cinnamon in the kitchen and the feeling of butter between my fingers while baking.

I caught myself thinking, *I want to bake something... just for me.* Not for a holiday, not for the kids, not for Tim. Just because I missed the way it made the house feel. Warm. Familiar. Safe.

That want was small—but it was mine.

And then I started to want to sit outside. To just sit. No phone. No noise. No pressure. Just me, the breeze, and maybe a mug of coffee that didn't go cold before I remembered to drink it. These weren't extravagant wants, but they were tender. Fragile. And for a woman who had lived years trying to stay invisible, even a small desire felt like cracking open.

Because deep down, wanting meant I still believed I deserved something.

But life wasn't tidy. It didn't rise in a perfect arc of healing.

Because just as I started to reach for more—just as I started wanting comfort, beauty, and joy again—everything around me reminded me that not everyone thought I deserved it.

My kids never accepted Tim.

Not from the beginning.

My daughter and oldest son made it clear that they wanted nothing to do with him. They never even gave him a chance. And while I tried not to take it personally, how could I not? When someone rejects the person who helped pull you out of your darkest place... it feels like they're rejecting you, too.

Tim never tried to be their father. He never forced anything. He loved me quietly, kindly. He helped where he could and gave me space where I needed it. But still, they hardened against him. Against us. And over time, the walls they built turned into silence.

I haven't spoken to my daughter or oldest son in years.

The grief of that runs deep.

The two younger boys have come around slowly. They visit now and then, and there are moments where it feels like maybe—just maybe—

CHAPTER 8

we can mend what's been broken. But there's always that tension, that sense of having to choose between my past and my present. Between who I used to be and the woman I'm still becoming.

And then there's my mom.

That wound is something else entirely.

She never accepted Tim either. From day one, she made that clear. She never saw what he gave me. She only saw who she thought I *should* be with—someone that made her more comfortable. Someone that didn't remind her of everything she didn't understand about me.

Our relationship was never easy. I was always the one giving, always the one trying to earn a place in her heart. But no matter what I did—how much I helped, how often I showed up—I always felt like I came in last.

Now that she's older—mid-80s, growing more bitter by the day—her cruelty cuts sharper than ever. There are days when I look at the woman who raised me and see only the damage she never admitted. The manipulation. The blame. The years of using me for what I could offer but never standing up for me when I needed her most.

Especially with Tim.

It got to the point where I couldn't keep trying. Couldn't keep bending myself in half just to avoid her wrath. I had to let her go. For my own sanity. For my peace. For the woman I was finally beginning to rediscover.

But the guilt still lingers sometimes. The voice in my head that says, *You're the daughter. You're supposed to try harder.* And then the other voice—stronger now—says, *You did try. You gave her everything. And it was never enough. Letting go doesn't mean you didn't love her. It means you finally started loving yourself.*

And in the middle of all that—Tim.

He's still here. Still loving me through it.

Even on days when I'm closed off. Even when I'm spiraling. Even when the pain of being rejected by the people I love most makes me cold and distant and hard to reach.

He stays.

He sees me.

He never asks me to be anyone but who I am in that exact moment.

That kind of love doesn't fix everything. But it sure softens the sharp edges.

Sometimes I sit with him in the quiet, my hand resting lightly on his, and think, *How is it possible that this man who was never wanted by my family became the only place I feel safe?*

And then the answer comes: *Because he never made me choose between who I was and who I am now.*

Still, the grief of not being accepted by my children… it's there. It sneaks up in the middle of the night. It shows up when I see other moms posting pictures of family dinners and holidays full of laughter and love. It hurts that my story isn't like that.

But I'm learning that even with that pain… I'm allowed to want joy. I'm allowed to want peace.

I don't have to earn it by fixing every broken relationship.

I can want it anyway.

The wanting is still quiet. Still cautious. Still tinged with fear. But it's here.

I want to bake again, not just for others—but for the little girl inside me who never got to feel comfort growing up.

I want to keep painting, even if no one else understands what it means to me.

I want to sit on the porch with Tim, sipping coffee and letting the sun hit my face, without apologizing for the life we've built in the shadows of so much disapproval.

I want to feel free in my body, even if it's been a battleground. I want to wear clothes that feel like me. I want to take care of myself because I

CHAPTER 8

deserve to feel good—not because someone else said I should.

I want to laugh again—real, belly-deep laughter that doesn't check the room first to make sure it's okay.

And I want to forgive myself for how long it took to start wanting again.

That quiet wanting isn't loud or flashy. It doesn't show up in grand gestures. It shows up in the way I reach for Tim's hand instead of pulling away. In the way I allow myself to make dinner feel special, even if it's just the two of us. In the way I keep a candle burning in the kitchen, even on hard days.

It shows up when I speak kindly to myself.

When I say, *You're allowed to want more.*

And I believe it.

Even if just a little.

Because after all these years of pain and rejection... that kind of believing is a beginning.

* * *

The weight didn't come all at once. It snuck in quietly, the way sorrow often does. One pound here. Five there. A tighter waistband. A shirt that didn't feel quite right. At first, I told myself it was stress. Trauma. Meds. Life. All of it true, but none of it softened the way I stared at myself in the mirror, feeling like I was watching a stranger slowly replace me.

I remember the first time I noticed I couldn't button a pair of jeans. I stood in my room, holding my breath, trying to will the denim to meet. When it didn't, I felt this sharp sting of shame—and immediately, I hated myself for it. I had been through so much. I had survived so much. Why was I letting something as small as a button undo me?

But it wasn't just the jeans. It was what they represented.

For years, I had lived in fight-or-flight. My body had been the battleground. First in my childhood, then in my marriage, then again after the assault. Every time something horrible happened, my body took the blow, and I never really stopped to thank it for carrying me through. I just wanted to disappear from it. I wanted out.

The meds didn't help. One prescription turned into another. Each one promising calm or sleep or relief from the gnawing anxiety, but they came with side effects that didn't care about my self-esteem. My appetite changed. My energy crashed. And the weight kept coming.

Before I knew it, I was over 300 pounds.

It didn't happen because I didn't care about myself. It happened because I was trying to survive. And for a long time, food was the one thing that didn't yell back. The one comfort that didn't ask anything of me. I could bake something, sit with it, feel full for a moment—and forget.

Forget the silence. Forget the fear. Forget the echo of being touched, used, and left shattered.

When people say "emotional eating," they often say it with a smirk. Like it's a weakness. But for me, food was a shield. It was soft when life had been hard. It was warm when the world had gone cold. And slowly, I started to wrap myself in it.

Layers of protection.

That's how I saw it.

Because deep down, there was something I never really admitted out loud until much later—I was afraid to lose the weight.

Terrified, actually.

The more invisible I became, the safer I felt. I hated the stares that used to follow me around. I hated the attention. I hated what came with being "seen." After everything I'd survived, I learned that being noticed often meant being in danger.

And so, I disappeared.

At least that's how it felt.

CHAPTER 8

People don't look the same way when you're heavy. Some ignore you altogether. Some look through you. Some make assumptions. But no one sees you as a target. No one reaches for you. No one sees your curves and wants to claim them. And in a way... that felt safe.

Safer than anything I'd known.

I hated how I looked, but I loved how I felt... protected. Dull. Tucked away from the world. It wasn't healthy, and I knew that. My body ached. My joints hurt. I was tired all the time. But I was also safe. And sometimes, safety felt more urgent than health.

Still, something inside me began to stir. Not loudly. Not in a way that demanded change. But gently. Whispering things like:

You deserve to feel better.

You deserve to walk without pain.

You deserve to live—not just exist.

And I wanted to believe that.

So, slowly, I began to change things. I started walking. Just a little at first. Around the block. Then again the next day. Then further. I changed what I was eating. I didn't restrict. I didn't starve. I just started caring again—not because I hated myself, but because I was tired of hurting.

It took years.

But I lost over 100 pounds.

And not one single person saw the fight behind that number.

They didn't see the nights I cried over a bowl of salad because it didn't taste like comfort. They didn't see the days I skipped meals because I was afraid I'd eat too much. They didn't see the shame. The guilt. The war inside my head every time the number on the scale shifted.

I did it mostly alone.

Tim was supportive, yes. He never made me feel less-than. Never commented on my size. Never once made me feel like I had to change to earn his love. But even with his support, this was a personal war. Because I wasn't just fighting calories. I was fighting history.

I was fighting a lifetime of trauma that taught me to stay small. To stay quiet. To disappear.

And now that the weight was coming off—I was terrified.

Terrified that people would see me again.

Terrified that the eyes would come back.

Terrified that the attention I worked so hard to avoid would find me.

So I stopped.

Right around the 100-pound mark, I paused everything. Not just physically—but mentally. I froze. Because deep down, I didn't want to keep going. I didn't want to be visible again. I didn't want to feel that fear crawl back up my spine every time someone looked at me too long.

I knew I still had weight to lose. Knew it would help my body. Knew it would be good for my health. But I couldn't make myself do it.

Because I didn't feel safe.

People praised me. Told me I looked amazing. Said I should be proud.

But I wasn't.

I was scared.

It felt like I was taking off my armor, one pound at a time—and I didn't know what to do with the skin underneath. The skin that had been touched without permission. The skin that remembered everything.

It was a strange thing—to be celebrated for something that made me feel so vulnerable. I wanted to scream, *You don't understand! This isn't a glow-up! This is terrifying!*

But instead, I smiled. Nodded. Said thank you.

And went home to cry.

Even now, I still live in that in-between space. I've kept the weight off, but I haven't lost much more. My body still carries extra pounds, and I still struggle with how I feel about it. Some days, I hate what I see. Other days, I'm grateful for the strength that body holds.

But always, beneath the layers, is that question:
Can I ever be thin and safe at the same time?
I don't know the answer yet.
But what I do know is this—I'm trying. I'm still here. I'm learning that maybe safety doesn't come from being invisible. Maybe it comes from reclaiming my space. From standing tall. From saying, *This is my body, and no one gets to hurt it anymore.*
Maybe I don't need to disappear to stay safe.
Maybe I just need to take up space in a new way. A stronger way. A way that honors everything I've been through.
And maybe, just maybe, one day—I'll keep going.
Not because I'm ashamed.
But because I'm ready.

* * *

It didn't come when I expected it. It never does, does it? Healing isn't something you can pencil into your calendar, or check off a to-do list like groceries or laundry. It arrives the way spring does after a brutal winter—soft at first, hesitant, like it's not sure it's welcome. And that's exactly how it felt the day I laughed.

Not a nervous laugh. Not a polite chuckle to fill awkward silence.

A real one.

It was the kind of laugh that cracked through years of tightness in my chest. The kind that made me clutch my stomach and wipe tears from my eyes afterward. The kind that startled me.

Because I didn't even know it was still in me.

It happened one ordinary afternoon, which somehow made it even more extraordinary. I was in the kitchen—where else? Tim was helping me put groceries away. He always messes up where things go, even after all these years. Somehow, he put the flour in the fridge, the maple syrup in the spice cabinet, and tried to wedge the eggs in sideways because "they fit better that way."

I turned around and caught him mid-cringe as the egg carton hit the floor and cracked open like a sad little grenade.

He looked at me, sheepish, like a boy who got caught sneaking cookies before dinner. And without thinking, without permission, a laugh escaped me.

It started small, like a bubbling inside my chest, and before I could stop it—it broke free.

And I just... laughed.

Hard.

I laughed at the eggs on the floor. I laughed at Tim's horrified face. I laughed at the absurdity of it all—how my life had once been filled with terror and pain and silence, and now here I was, in a little kitchen, laughing over broken eggs with a man who loved me through everything.

Tim stood there, blinking, not sure what to do. And then he laughed too. Not just because it was funny, but because I was laughing. He looked at me like I'd just given him a gift he didn't expect.

And in a way, I had.

Because for the longest time, I hadn't laughed like that. I hadn't allowed myself to. It felt like laughing was a betrayal of everything I'd been through. Like if I let myself feel light, it meant I was forgetting. And I didn't want to forget. I didn't want to dishonor the version of me who crawled her way through the darkest years.

But in that moment—standing in flour-dusted slippers, laughing with tears running down my cheeks—I realized something:

Laughter wasn't betrayal.

It was proof.

Proof that I had survived.

Proof that there was still something inside me that hadn't given up.

CHAPTER 8

That even in the wreckage, I had carried a spark forward. Something sacred. Something untouched.

And maybe, just maybe, I was ready to let it breathe again.

That laugh stayed with me all day. It hovered in my chest like a warm glow. I smiled at nothing while folding laundry. I hummed while stirring a pot of soup. I lit a candle that evening and let the scent of cinnamon and vanilla swirl around the room like a hug.

I felt... almost like myself again. Or maybe like someone new. Someone softer. Someone who knew that joy could exist in the same room as grief. That you could hold both.

That night, after the kitchen was clean and the lights were low, I curled up on the couch with Tim, blanket over my legs, and said quietly, "I laughed today."

He looked at me, smiling. "I know. It was beautiful."

And I cried.

Not because I was sad. But because he noticed. Because that laugh wasn't lost. It mattered. And someone saw it. Held space for it. Celebrated it.

That was the first one. The first real laugh.

It wasn't the last, though. Slowly, gently, they started to come more often. During funny shows. While baking something that went hilariously wrong. During quiet conversations with Tim where we let our guards down and just spoke freely.

I didn't need an audience. I didn't need a stage. I just needed these quiet little pockets of safety, where joy could rise without fear.

But even as I started to laugh more, there was always that tiny flicker of guilt. A little whisper that said, *Do you really deserve this? After everything?*

And I had to talk back to that voice.

I had to say, *Yes. I do.*

Because laughter doesn't mean I'm healed. It doesn't erase the past.

It doesn't rewrite the trauma. It just means I'm living again.

That I'm choosing to stay.

And that's brave.

Sometimes, when I laugh now, it still surprises me. Like catching a reflection in the mirror that looks a little like the old me—the girl who used to dance in the kitchen, who used to plan silly birthday parties and sing off-key on purpose.

She's not all the way back.

But she's peeking through.

And I think she's proud of me.

Tim has become a witness to this slow return of my joy. He never pushes. He never asks for more than I can give. But I see the way his eyes light up when I smile for real. The way his hand lingers on mine when I'm telling a story and my voice gets stronger.

He's seen all the versions of me.

The hollow one.

The angry one.

The numb one.

And now, this one—the version of me that's trying to laugh again. Trying to live again.

And he's never wavered.

Sometimes, I think that's what love really is—not the big declarations or the fancy dates. But the quiet presence. The way someone holds your hand while you relearn how to breathe. The way they sit beside you when you're silent for hours. The way they catch your laughter and hold it like it's something sacred.

Because it is.

It's sacred.

That laugh? It was freeing.

It wasn't loud. It wasn't long.

But it was real.

CHAPTER 8

And that made it everything.

These days, I still cry sometimes. I still battle flashbacks. I still have nights when I sleep on the couch with a blanket pulled tight and all the lights on. But I also have days where I laugh. Days where I hum while baking. Days where I lean into Tim's shoulder and let my body remember what it feels like to rest.

I've learned that healing isn't linear. It's not a finish line you cross.

It's a laugh in a kitchen full of broken eggs.

It's a candle burning at the end of a long day.

It's saying, *I'm still here,* even when everything inside you once begged you to disappear.

So yes, I laughed.

And I'll keep laughing, when I can.

Because each time I do—it's another stitch in the torn fabric of my life. Another step toward the woman I'm still becoming.

And I love her.

Because she didn't give up.

Chapter 9

He sent the friend request.

That's how it started—not with a grand gesture or a swoon-worthy moment. Just a quiet notification in my Facebook inbox one day. His name didn't ring a bell at first, but I noticed we had a mutual connection—my sister. That's what made me accept it. Nothing more, nothing less. It was just another face among the many on my friends list. No conversation. No likes. No messages. For a whole year, he stayed silent.

And honestly, so did I.

Then, one day, something in me cracked open—just enough to leak a little bit of my sadness onto the screen. I made a simple post. Something like, *"Feeling sad today. Not really sure why."* Just a few words, really. I didn't expect a response. I was used to posting into the void. Most people scroll past heartache unless it comes wrapped in humor or flowers.

But then he commented.

It wasn't overbearing or invasive. Just a phone number. And an offer.

"If you need someone to talk to, I'm here."

I remember staring at it, unsure what to feel. I wasn't good at trusting people. Especially not men. Especially not strangers. My instinct was to retreat—to shut the laptop, go dark, crawl deeper into my safe little cave of silence. And I almost did.

CHAPTER 9

But right as I went to log out, my chat popped open.

One word.

"Hi."

It was him.

I froze.

I stared at that one syllable for way too long. My heart was pounding. I didn't know him. I didn't owe him a response. But there was something so soft about it. No pressure. No manipulation. Just a quiet *hello*.

So I answered.

And that one word turned into hours of conversation.

I don't know how to explain it except to say—it felt like exhaling for the first time in a long time. Like there was no expectation. Just space. Just someone listening. I hadn't realized how much I missed that—just being heard. Being seen without someone trying to fix me or talk over me or make it about them.

We talked every day after that.

And I don't mean the quick, surface-level kind of chatter most people exchange. I mean deep conversations that stretched long into the night. We talked about our childhoods. About music. About heartbreak. About what scared us. What made us laugh. It didn't feel like flirting. It felt like finally being understood.

And I needed that more than I even realized.

A month later, he got on a Greyhound bus in Alabama and rode for hours to come be with me.

It sounds impulsive when I say it like that—maybe even reckless. But at the time, it didn't feel that way. It felt right. He had nowhere anchoring him. I was drowning in loneliness and fear. We had built something rare in a short time—an emotional intimacy I'd never really known. And when he stepped off that bus, I felt... terrified.

He moved in, but for the first three or four months, I could barely talk to him. Not because of who he was—but because of everything I had been through. I was scared. Guarded. Damaged. My walls were built high and thick for survival, and he had walked into a war zone he didn't even know existed. Every time he tried to get close, my instincts told me to pull away. Every kind gesture made me suspicious. Every smile made me panic a little.

I didn't know how to be loved anymore.

Tim was patient. But eventually, even he began to feel the weight of it. I remember the day he asked me, point blank, *"Do you want me to leave?"*

He wasn't being dramatic. He just felt unwanted. Like a ghost in my life. Like someone crashing a party that hadn't really started yet.

That question hit me hard.

Because I didn't want him to leave.

I just didn't know how to let him in.

I'd been surviving on my own for so long, it felt impossible to believe that someone might love me without strings. Without hurting me. Without turning into someone else once I let my guard down. I didn't trust it. I didn't trust *him*—not because he wasn't trustworthy, but because my trauma didn't allow space for trust.

Still, I didn't want him to go.

So I said so. Quietly. Clumsily. But honestly.

And Tim... he stayed.

He didn't push. He didn't guilt me. He just kept showing up in the small ways. Sitting beside me in silence when I couldn't speak. Washing the dishes when I didn't ask. Making coffee. Turning on soft music in the background. He waited until I felt safe enough to come closer.

And I did.

Slowly.

Not in some sweeping movie moment—but in a million small steps. I let him bring me coffee in the morning. I let him see me cry. I let him hear my stories. I let him touch my hand without flinching. I let him hug me for real, not the stiff kind you give people out of politeness. I let him into my world—my real world, with all its shadows and edges and broken parts.

It wasn't easy. It wasn't neat. But it was real.

We built a life from those pieces. Not a perfect life. Not even always a peaceful one. But a life rooted in truth. In honesty. In choosing each other every day.

That was twelve years ago.

And even now, I look at him and think about how close I came to missing it. If I hadn't answered that "hi." If I had let fear win. If I had stayed behind the wall forever.

But I didn't.

He knocked.

And this time, I opened the door.

Not all at once. Not without hesitation. But I opened it.

And inside, I found something I thought I'd never have again.

Someone who didn't want to fix me or save me—just love me exactly as I was.

And that's where the real healing began.

* * *

I didn't realize how much of me I'd hidden away until someone tried to truly *see* me.

Not the surface stuff—the polite smiles, the nervous small talk, the day-to-day routines that keep things looking fine from the outside. I'm talking about the deep-down, trembling parts. The places in me that hadn't been touched in years, not because they weren't there, but because they had been buried under fear, shame, and years of survival.

When Tim moved in, I didn't let him see those parts right away. I couldn't. My body, my mind, my very spirit was on high alert. Trauma teaches you early how to become invisible. How to stay guarded. How to shape-shift into whatever feels safest at the time. So for the first few months, that's what I did. I existed behind a kind of invisible glass. Present, but distant. Speaking, but not really connecting. Smiling, but only with half my heart.

It wasn't because I didn't care. It was because I cared too much—and I didn't trust what would happen if I let him in.

I remember one morning in particular. It had been a rough night—one of those where sleep only comes in ten-minute waves between the tossing and turning and the constant check-ins with the locked door. I'd gotten up before him and was sitting at the kitchen table, still in my old oversized shirt, hair wild, no makeup, puffy eyes from the weight of life. And he came out, eyes still heavy from sleep, and smiled at me like I was something soft and beautiful.

I remember thinking: *How can he look at me like that?* Didn't he see the mess? The exhaustion? The damage?

But he didn't look away.

He walked over, kissed the top of my head, and poured me a cup of coffee. No words. Just presence. And that, I think, is when I started to crack open.

Tim didn't come with demands. He didn't show up expecting me to be someone I wasn't. He didn't try to fix me, or preach at me, or dismiss the things I struggled with. He just... showed up. Over and over again. In tiny, steady ways.

And that's what slowly made me feel safe enough to be seen.

I remember the first time I let myself cry in front of him—really cry. Not the silent tears you sneak in the bathroom. Not the quick wipe-away before someone notices. I'm talking sobbing. Ugly crying. The kind where everything in you caves in for a minute.

CHAPTER 9

It was over something small, honestly. I was cooking dinner and dropped a glass dish. It shattered across the kitchen floor, and I froze. Just stood there staring at the pieces, the sound still ringing in my ears. He rushed in, asking if I was okay, and I just broke. I dropped to the floor, hands shaking, and all that fear and exhaustion came pouring out. I couldn't stop it. I couldn't explain it. I just sat there, crying harder than I had in a long, long time.

And Tim? He didn't rush to clean up. He didn't try to get me to stop crying. He sat down right next to me on that tile floor and held me. Gently. Quietly. Like someone who understood that this wasn't just about a broken dish.

It was about being broken.

And for the first time, it felt like someone was willing to sit with me in that brokenness.

That kind of tenderness… it undoes you.

Over the next few weeks, I found myself loosening. Not all at once. But in small ways. I started talking more—about my past, about the pieces I was most ashamed of. I told him about the night the intruder came. About the way my body had become a battleground I didn't always feel safe in. About the times I locked myself in the bathroom and cried so hard I couldn't breathe. I told him things I'd never told another soul.

And he didn't flinch.

He listened. Sometimes with tears in his own eyes. Sometimes with nothing but a hand on mine and a stillness in his breath like he was trying to carry some of it with me.

He made it okay to speak.

He made it okay to be soft again.

But it wasn't just emotional intimacy that scared me—it was physical closeness, too.

For so long, my body had been something to survive. Something to hide. Something to protect at all costs. It had been violated. Shamed.

Touched without consent. It had carried babies, carried trauma, carried weight I didn't know how to shed—both literally and emotionally.

When you've been through what I have, it's hard to let anyone close, even someone you love.

And Tim knew that.

He never pushed. Never made me feel like my worth was tied to what I could give physically. He made space for the slowness. For the healing. For the relearning.

And little by little, I let him in.

The first time I let him touch my face, really touch it, I remember thinking, *He's going to see everything.* All the fine lines. All the stress. All the years I spent hiding. But he didn't see what I feared. He saw *me*. And he held me like someone who didn't want to take anything—just to offer comfort. To offer love.

It was terrifying.

But it was healing.

Over time, the things I once hid became shared spaces. I stopped turning off the light when I changed my clothes. I let him brush my hair. I let him bring me tea while I was in the tub. I let him trace the stretch marks on my stomach and kiss them like they were holy.

He made me feel like my body wasn't something to apologize for.

He made me feel like I was still lovable—even in the places I didn't love myself yet.

There was one night, not too long after we'd really begun letting each other in, where I asked him: *"Why did you stay when I barely spoke to you for months?"*

He looked at me, so steady, and said, *"Because I knew you were still in there. I was waiting for her to come back."*

And I think that was the moment I knew this wasn't just some rebound connection. This was a man who saw me—*really* saw me—and didn't run.

CHAPTER 9

He didn't need me to be shiny and healed and whole.

He just needed me to be real.

And so I kept showing up.

Even on the days I wanted to hide.

Even on the nights the flashbacks came and I needed space to breathe.

Even when I felt ugly and unworthy and weighed down with memories.

He never asked me to be more.

He never asked me to be less.

He just asked me to be myself.

And in doing that, he gave me the space to rediscover who that was.

He saw all of me—and stayed.

That kind of love?

It's rare.

It's raw.

It's not built on perfection or fairy tale expectations. It's built on quiet mornings. On cups of coffee shared in silence. On tears that fall without warning. On laughter that catches you off guard. On two people choosing each other, again and again even when one of them doesn't feel like they deserve to be chosen.

I had spent so much of my life believing I was too broken to be loved like that.

But I wasn't.

I was just waiting for the right heart to see me.

And now, years later, I still thank God for that Facebook message. For that "hi" that turned into a life. For the man who saw the darkest parts of me and didn't turn away.

Because when Tim saw all of me—really saw me—it taught me something I'd been needing to learn for a long time:

I was never too far gone.

I was never too broken.

I was just waiting to be seen with love instead of fear. And that's exactly what he gave me.

* * *

Building a life after trauma isn't like building a fresh house on an empty lot—it's more like trying to make a home out of rubble. You're sorting through what's left, deciding what you can salvage and what you have to let go of. You're learning how to live again, but nothing about it is easy or neat or simple.

When Tim came into my life, I didn't magically become healed or whole or fearless. I was still carrying my baggage—years of it. The kind you don't pack into a suitcase, but the kind that weighs down your soul. And he brought his, too. Because that's the thing—none of us get through life without a few bruises, a few scars of our own. But the miracle, I guess, was that we were willing to lay them out in the open and say, "Here's what I've got. Can we work with this?"

And we did. Somehow, we did.

At first, building that life together looked really quiet. It wasn't fancy or picture-perfect. It was burnt toast and awkward silences. It was me retreating into myself when a sound startled me, and him learning that I needed time, not questions. It was late nights with the TV on low because neither of us could sleep. It was him bringing me coffee in my favorite chipped mug and me remembering how to laugh at his dry jokes.

We didn't start with a wedding or a ring or a white-picket fence. We started with folding laundry together. With figuring out how to share the bathroom. With him patiently waiting as I navigated what it meant to trust someone again.

It was hard for me. I'd been through so much—too much. The kind of pain that reshapes how you see the world. And loving someone, really

CHAPTER 9

letting them in, felt dangerous. Vulnerable. But Tim never made me feel small for that. He never rushed me. He never made my healing about him.

He made space for me to grow. At my own pace. In my own way.

We found rhythms in our days—simple, steady ones. I'd make breakfast; He'd help me wash the dishes. We'd sit together in the living room, each doing our own thing, but together. There was no pressure to always talk. Sometimes we were just two people sharing the same air, and that was enough.

But over time, the conversations deepened.

We started dreaming out loud. Talking about little things—what we'd plant in a garden if we had one, where we'd want to go if we ever took a trip, what kind of dog we'd adopt if life ever made space for one. And in those little moments, those half-whispered dreams, I started to see what we were really building.

A life. Not perfect. Not polished. But real.

It wasn't just healing for me. It was healing for him too.

Tim had his own wounds. Things he didn't always talk about. But I could see them in the way he carried himself—in the way he flinched at raised voices, in the way he struggled with feeling worthy of love. We were both people who had been broken in our own ways. But where that could have created distance, it brought us closer. We recognized something in each other.

Not brokenness, exactly. But resilience.

We were both still standing, after everything. And maybe that was something sacred.

The hard part was letting go of what the world thought we were supposed to be.

My family didn't accept him. Not really. My mom never gave him a fair chance. She never really gave *me* one, either. She treated me like I was always too much and never enough all at once. Even when she was cruel, I still longed for her approval—for her to say, "I'm proud of you. I see you." But that never came. And when I chose Tim, I think she saw that as a betrayal.

My daughter and my oldest son stopped speaking to me. And that? That tore something open in me that still hasn't quite closed.

I wanted them to see him the way I did—to see the way he looked at me like I was still beautiful, even when I felt like nothing. To see how he would warm up my tea if he noticed it had gone cold. How he remembered all the little things I said, even when I didn't realize I was saying them. How he stood by me when most people would have run.

But they didn't want to see that.

They had already made up their minds.

It hurt. Deeply. And there were nights I would lie awake and wonder if I had done something wrong by choosing love over obligation. But then Tim would stir beside me, reach for my hand without saying a word, and I'd remember: this love was real. And that mattered more than appearances.

My two younger boys came around, slowly. They saw the way Tim showed up. No flash, no manipulation. Just steady, quiet care. They started to visit more. Share meals with us. Laugh a little louder. And I clung to that—those small bridges being rebuilt.

Even still, it's hard.

We live in this world that says family is everything. But what do you do when the people who share your blood are the ones who hurt you most?

What do you do when you've spent your whole life trying to be seen by them and it still isn't enough?

You build a new family.

Not to replace the old one, but to remind yourself that love doesn't have to come from pain. That family isn't always blood—it's who shows up. It's who stays. It's who sees you in the mess and says, "I'm not

CHAPTER 9

going anywhere."

And that's what Tim did.

There were days I still struggled—still wanted to pull away, hide, numb out. But he stayed. He never made my healing a burden. He never made me feel like I was too broken to love.

And I think that's the most important part of this whole thing. You can survive alone. I had. For years. But building a life—one with joy and softness and laughter—that takes trust. That takes letting someone hold a piece of your story without dropping it.

We started doing things together. Little traditions that grounded us. Country drives on Sunday afternoons. Pancakes on Sunday mornings. Listening to old music while barbequing. He'd pick me roses from our rose garden when I had a rough day, and I'd make his favorite beans and cornbread when the weather turned cold.

We carved out a life that looked nothing like anyone else's—but it fit us.

And somehow, in the middle of that, I started to feel like maybe I wasn't surviving anymore.

Maybe I was living.

Don't get me wrong—it wasn't all sunshine. We had our moments. Times I'd shut down and he wouldn't know how to reach me. Times he'd get quiet and I'd feel rejected even though it had nothing to do with me. But we learned how to talk through those things. To say, "I'm not okay, but I want to be here." That matters.

We fought, sure. But we fought *for* each other, not against.

That makes all the difference.

We created something together. Something steady. Something kind.

And years later—twelve of them now—I still look at him and think, *Thank God I answered that message. Thank God I didn't let fear win.*

Because the life we built? It may not be what I imagined as a little girl. But it's something better in a lot of ways. It's real. It's rooted. It's soft.

I never thought I'd find safety in someone else's arms.

But I did.

And even now, after all these years, there are nights when we lie in bed, and I still reach for his hand before I fall asleep—not because I'm afraid, but because I want to remember what it feels like to be held. To be chosen. To be loved, fully and without condition.

Tim knocked on the door of my life when I had nearly given up on letting anyone in.

And I'm so glad I answered.

Chapter 10

There was a time in my life when I couldn't enter a room without first scanning for exits. When every creak in the floor sent my heart racing and every quiet moment felt more like a setup than a blessing. But somehow, despite all of that, the kitchen became my safe place. It didn't happen all at once—it happened slowly, almost without me noticing. One moment at a time. One ritual layered gently over another. And before I knew it, the kitchen wasn't just where I cooked anymore—it was where I found peace.

It began with the spices.

Maybe that seems small, but when you've lived in chaos—when your body is constantly braced for something bad to happen—there's something deeply healing about taking control of even the smallest corner of your world. The spice cabinet had always been a mess. Random bottles crammed in sideways, duplicates of cinnamon and paprika because I'd forget I already had them. Old dusty jars in the back that hadn't been touched in years. It was a cluttered, noisy little space that felt like a mirror of my mind.

One day, on a quiet afternoon, I opened that cabinet and just stared at it. Something in me whispered, "Let's fix this." Not because I had to. Not because anyone was coming over or because I needed a specific spice for a recipe. I just needed to do something that felt like order. Like calm. Like care.

So I pulled everything out, lined it all across the counter. I took a damp cloth and wiped every shelf, every sticky ring left behind by years of reaching for flavor. I looked at each label, each expiration date, and I let go of what was no longer good. There was something almost beautiful in it. As if each jar I wiped clean, each bottle I relabeled, was a small act of reclaiming myself. Sorting spices became a ritual, a way of saying, "This space matters. I matter."

I bought matching jars. Not fancy, just simple clear ones with little labels. One for cinnamon. One for oregano. One for cloves, which I hardly used but loved the smell of. I lined them up by height, by alphabet, by purpose. I stood back and looked at them when I was done, and for the first time in a long time, something inside me settled. That tiny cabinet of order was mine. No chaos. No fear. Just spices—organized and waiting.

From there, it grew.

Baking had always been something I enjoyed, but now it became something deeper. It became sacred. It became prayer.

There's something about baking that calls for presence. You can't rush it. You have to soften the butter. You have to stir gently. You have to wait for dough to rise, for flavors to bloom. It grounds you. And in those early days, when I couldn't quiet my mind long enough to pray in the traditional way, I began to pray with flour on my hands.

I'd whisper prayers as I kneaded bread—pressing hope into the dough with every motion. "Keep them safe," I'd murmur under my breath, folding it over. "Let this be enough." "Help me feel okay again." And it wasn't just words—it was intention. It was presence. It was giving myself over to the moment with all the love and all the ache inside me.

Measuring sugar, cracking eggs, waiting for the oven to preheat—it became more than cooking. It became healing. And there was comfort in knowing that no matter how broken I felt inside, if I followed the recipe, something beautiful would come out of it. Even when I was unsure about everything else in life, I could be sure that 350 degrees for 28 minutes would give me warm, soft cookies that filled the house with a smell that felt like safety.

There were days when I didn't even want to eat what I baked. I just wanted to create it. To watch it rise. To pull it from the oven and see that it worked. That I worked. That something was still good in the world.

And the music—oh, the music. It came back like a whisper first. Just a little background sound to drown out the quiet, to push away the anxiety that silence used to bring. But then it turned into something more.

There was a morning I'll never forget. The kids were still asleep, the house was cool and dim, and I had just finished mixing a batch of cinnamon bread. I'd tucked it in a warm spot to rise and felt that familiar itch to clean up the counters, to wipe down the sink, to make everything nice. On a whim, I turned on the radio—just low, something soft. And then, like magic, the right song came on. One of those songs that carries memory in its melody. Something from before. From when life was simple and I was still whole.

I stood there with the sponge in one hand, the scent of cinnamon in the air, and I just let the music move through me. I hummed along. I wiped the counter in rhythm. I felt my shoulders drop for the first time in weeks. That moment—music, motion, scent, warmth—it was like all the parts of me lined up again. Just for a second. Just enough.

After that, music became a part of everything. Not because I needed to fill the silence anymore—but because it brought life into the space. I played oldies when I cleaned. Worship songs when I baked bread. Sometimes jazz when I was organizing, just to feel fancy. The music turned the kitchen from just another room into something sacred. It wrapped around me while I moved, reminded me that joy still existed, that rhythm still pulsed somewhere beneath the weight I carried.

Sometimes I'd dance a little while stirring a pot. Not a full dance—

just a sway of the hips, a tap of the foot. But it was enough. Enough to feel alive again. Enough to feel like myself.

I think that's what the kitchen gave me most of all: pieces of myself.

In the world outside that room, I still felt nervous. Still jumped at sounds. Still checked the locks too many times. Still didn't trust my reflection in the mirror. But in the kitchen, I started to believe I was still in there somewhere. That even though trauma had taken so much from me, it hadn't taken everything.

It didn't take the way my hands knew how to braid a loaf of challah.

It didn't take the way music made my shoulders loosen.

It didn't take the way a clean kitchen towel laid over warm rolls brought me comfort.

And it didn't take the way organizing something small—like a drawer of tea bags or a collection of cookie cutters—could bring peace into the middle of a storm.

The kitchen became a kind of sanctuary. A chapel made of tile and flour and music. A place where I didn't have to perform. Where I didn't have to explain. Where I could cry into a mixing bowl and stir through the ache. Where I could taste something sweet and remember that goodness still existed.

I remember one night after the kids had gone to bed. The dishes were done, the lights were low, and I stood at the stove stirring a pot of something warm and simple—maybe soup or apples with cinnamon, I don't even remember. But the windows fogged up from the steam, and I could see my reflection—soft and shadowed—in the glass. And I thought, "This is healing, too."

Not the big moments. Not the therapy breakthroughs or the court hearings or the well-meaning advice from others.

This.

This quiet stir. This warm kitchen. This playlist humming behind me. This soft light. This rhythm of hands in motion. This choosing to

CHAPTER 10

bake even when my heart felt raw. This choosing to clean even when my mind felt messy. This choosing to show up for myself in a room that once just meant obligation—but now meant restoration.

Sometimes healing doesn't look like triumph. Sometimes it looks like labeling spice jars.

Sometimes it looks like letting music carry you through a rough afternoon.

Sometimes it looks like kneading bread with tears in your eyes and love in your heart.

And that's what the kitchen became for me—not just a room, but a witness. A partner. A space where I slowly began to trust myself again. A space where I could remember who I was and who I was becoming.

Even now, years later, when I walk barefoot into that room in the early morning light, before the world fully wakes up, I still feel it—that sacred hum. The way the light hits the counter. The way the cupboards creak when I open them. The soft shuffle of pulling out a pan. The sound of a spoon against a ceramic bowl.

It's all familiar. It's all safe.

And maybe it was never just about the food. Maybe it was about presence. About reclaiming what was mine. About finding small, everyday ways to come back to myself.

Because healing isn't always loud. It isn't always seen.

Sometimes it's a drawer full of neatly stacked measuring spoons.

Sometimes it's a loaf of bread rising on the counter.

Sometimes it's music playing while you wipe crumbs off the floor.

And sometimes, it's just standing still in the middle of your kitchen... and realizing, I'm okay here.

I'm safe here.

I'm home.

* * *

It's funny how the smallest things—quiet, ordinary things—end up saving you.

After everything I had lived through, I didn't trust much anymore. Not people. Not places. Not even my own instincts, sometimes. But there were certain routines, certain tiny rhythms in my day, that began to hold me. They didn't ask much from me. They didn't expect me to be healed or whole or even okay. They just let me show up as I was—tired, worn, hollow, afraid—and gave me a place to land.

One of those routines was the way I washed the dishes.

I used to rush through it, back when life felt busier and my thoughts didn't chase me through every room. But after the trauma, everything shifted. Time felt different. I couldn't multitask anymore. My brain couldn't handle the noise. I needed slow. I needed simple. I needed something with structure that wouldn't collapse on me. So I stopped rushing the dishes.

I started doing them one by one.

Each plate, each fork, each glass—I held them in my hands like they were sacred. The warm water, the soft swirl of bubbles, the sound of the sponge against ceramic—those were the things I could count on. And in a world where my mind felt like a maze of panic and memory, that consistency meant everything.

Sometimes I'd hum quietly while I worked. Sometimes I didn't make a sound at all. I'd let the water run over my fingers and try to breathe slow. Try to remember I was here. That this was now. That I was safe.

The kitchen window above the sink became a sort of companion. I'd stare out of it while I rinsed each plate, watching the seasons pass on the other side of the glass. Bare branches. Blossoming buds. Rain streaking down in tiny rivers. Snowflakes landing and melting in an instant. That window grounded me. It reminded me that life kept moving, even when I felt stuck.

There were days I cried into that sink. Silent tears slipping down as the water ran, mixing in with the soap and the crumbs from breakfast. And there were days I didn't cry, but just stood there—numb, disconnected—but still washing, still rinsing, still placing things in the drying rack. And even that—just *doing*—was enough.

That routine didn't fix me. But it held me. It gave me something steady to return to. It was the kind of quiet ritual that asked for nothing but presence. And for a woman who was used to being afraid of the stillness, it helped me make peace with it.

In the evenings, once the dishes were stacked, once the kitchen was wiped down and the day had been folded into bedtime routines and dimmed lights, I'd turn to another routine that began to hold me: evening tea.

I never used to drink tea at night. I was always a morning coffee person, rushing through the day on caffeine and obligation. But somewhere along the way—maybe during a particularly sleepless stretch of nights—I found myself craving warmth without noise. Something quiet. Gentle. Something that didn't jolt me awake, but coaxed me toward rest.

So I started making tea before bed.

At first, it was just a bag of chamomile in hot water. Simple. Easy. But then I began to turn it into more. I'd light a candle. I'd pick out a mug I loved—usually one with chipped paint or a floral print that reminded me of my grandmother. I'd pour the boiling water slowly, watching the steam curl into the air like a prayer. And then I'd wrap both hands around the cup and sit in the silence.

That cup became something of a confession booth. It held more than herbs and water—it held the weight of the day. The things I couldn't say out loud. The ache in my chest. The questions I still didn't have answers to. The anger that lingered even after years. The grief that still showed up in strange, sudden ways.

Some nights I'd sit in the quiet with that cup and let the heat settle into my bones. Other nights I'd play soft music. Sometimes I'd journal. Sometimes I'd just sit with my thoughts, even when they made me uncomfortable. It was my way of unwinding—not just my body, but my soul. Of telling myself, "You made it through another day. That's enough. Rest now."

And while the dishes and the tea comforted me in quiet, solitary ways—there was another rhythm that began to hold me in a more tender, shared way: cooking for Tim.

When he first came into my life, I was still learning how to trust again. I was cautious. Protective of my space, my kids, my mind. But there was something about the way he showed up—gentle, consistent, never rushing me—that softened a part of me I didn't know was still reachable.

And it was in the kitchen where I learned to let him in.

I started cooking for him before I even realized it meant something. A hearty stew on a cold night. Pancakes on a lazy weekend morning. Simple things. Comfortable things. But over time, those meals became a language between us. A way to say, "I care about you." A way to say, "This space is safe. This table is shared. You belong here."

There was one evening I'll never forget. I'd made pork chops—nothing fancy, just browned in a skillet with a bit of garlic and brown sugar—and I watched him take that first bite. His eyes lit up like a kid. He looked at me and said, "This tastes like something my mom used to make." And then he smiled—one of those soft, sincere smiles that felt like sunlight breaking through.

It caught me off guard, that smile. Not because it was unusual, but because it made me feel... seen. Like all the effort I put into that meal—choosing the right spices, making sure it wasn't overdone, setting the table—wasn't invisible.

Cooking for Tim became something steady in my life. Something I looked forward to. Not in the performative sense, not in the way I once felt obligated to show up for people who didn't really care—but in a sacred, quiet, generous way. It felt like giving him a piece of my heart that I could serve on a plate. Something I had chosen, prepared, poured myself into.

And it brought a kind of healing I didn't expect.

Because in feeding him, I was also feeding the part of myself that wanted to believe in goodness again. In kindness. In love that didn't take. Love that didn't hurt. Love that lingered at the kitchen table long after the plates were cleared.

We'd talk while I stirred sauces. He'd keep me company while I chopped vegetables. Sometimes he'd even help—peeling potatoes, washing lettuce, making me laugh in the middle of chopping onions so I'd mess it all up and start again. We were building something in that space—not just meals, but memories. Rituals. Trust.

There were nights we didn't talk much. Nights when the day had worn us down. But I'd still cook. I'd still serve. And he'd still smile that soft smile, still say, "This is amazing," even if it was just leftovers or a sandwich thrown together at the last minute.

Because he understood. He saw the care behind it. The love. The effort.

He saw *me*.

And in return, I saw myself through his eyes—someone capable, someone nurturing, someone worthy.

The kitchen, in all its quiet rituals, became the thread that stitched me back together. Washing dishes slowly reminded me I could create calm. Evening tea reminded me I could create comfort. Cooking for Tim reminded me I could create connection.

None of those routines were loud or flashy. They didn't cure my PTSD. They didn't erase the fear. But they gave me a place to breathe. A rhythm to hold onto. A daily reminder that I wasn't as lost as I thought I was.

Because healing doesn't always come in big moments. Sometimes it comes in warm water and lemon tea. In cinnamon and garlic. In a table set for two.

Sometimes it comes in silence.

Sometimes it comes in song.

Sometimes it comes in letting someone you trust eat the first bite and watching the joy bloom across their face.

And sometimes, healing comes when you least expect it—at the end of a long day, standing barefoot in the kitchen, realizing that despite everything you've lost, you're still here.

You're still showing up.

You're still creating something soft and sacred in the middle of a life that once felt too broken to touch.

The kitchen didn't fix me. But it held me while I did the work.

And maybe that's what sacred spaces do—they don't demand that you be whole. They simply make room for your pieces. They cradle you in the quiet. They teach you to trust again. To love again. To taste again.

And for me, it started with soap suds and a teacup.

And a man who said thank you.

* * *

There's something sacred about a woman's hands in the kitchen.

Not in the romanticized way people talk about "housewives" from a distance, not in the polished, Pinterest-perfect version of homemaking that shows up in glossy photos—but in the real, raw, sometimes tired, sometimes tearful rhythm of preparing dinner when no one's watching.

I don't think I always realized it, but now I see it clearly: the divine shows up in the chopping of onions, in the folding of napkins, in the quiet hum of the oven preheating. I used to think holiness only existed in churches or scripture or worship music. But I've come to believe that God moves through the ordinary too. Through hands that stir soup. Through a woman who wakes up every morning and makes something out of very little—again and again.

That realization didn't come to me in a flash. It came slowly, like the rising of bread in a warm kitchen—quiet, patient, unassuming. There was no lightning bolt. Just dinner prep.

It was one of those evenings where the day had worn me thin. Tim was still at work, the house was quiet except for the low hum of the fridge, and I stood at the counter with the cutting board in front of me. My hands moved on instinct—peeling carrots, slicing them into coins, the way I'd done a thousand times before. The kitchen light was soft, yellow. My feet were sore. My heart was heavy. I didn't feel like praying, didn't feel like reading scripture. But as I stood there, doing the simple work of feeding the man I love, something shifted.

The tears came quietly—not loud or gasping, but warm and slow, like rain down the cheeks. I didn't even know why at first. I just stood there with the knife in one hand and a half-chopped onion in the other, and it felt like the heaviness cracked open just enough for God to slip in.

That's when I realized I was praying.

Not with words. Not out loud. But with every movement of my hands. Every slice, every stir, every little detail I put into that meal—it was all a form of worship. A form of surrender. A form of love. There's divinity in that kind of offering. In showing up to feed someone when you're tired. In pouring your heart into a stew or a pan of cornbread or a plate of roasted vegetables, even when you're unsure what tomorrow holds.

Dinner prep became holy.

It wasn't just about feeding our bodies. It was about grounding myself in something real. In something that didn't require performance or perfection. It was the one part of my day where I didn't have to pretend. I could just *be*. The me who was healing. The me who was weary. The me who didn't have all the answers, but who still had a pantry of love to draw from.

There's something sacred about a well-worn kitchen. The scent of garlic hitting butter in a hot pan. The clatter of a wooden spoon on the edge of a pot. The hush that settles over the house when dinner's almost done and the people you love are on their way home. That's the rhythm I started to live in.

Over time, the routine itself became a kind of purpose.

In the early years after trauma, I often felt like I was floating—disconnected from the world, from my own body, from joy. But routine gave me an anchor. It was simple, yes, but powerful. Knowing what I was going to do at 4:00 p.m. gave structure to the chaos. Knowing I needed to thaw meat or wash rice gave me something tangible to focus on. And slowly, I began to build a kind of peace around that consistency.

There's something deeply healing in repetition.

Some people might see it as boring—doing the same tasks, the same meals, the same rhythms day after day. But for me, it was life-saving. It brought order to what had once felt like chaos. And it reminded me that I could create something meaningful, something nurturing, even when I felt like a mess inside.

Cooking didn't ask me to be perfect. It just asked me to be present.

And in that presence, I found purpose.

It wasn't flashy. It didn't come with applause or recognition. But I knew that when I chopped those vegetables, when I marinated that chicken, when I buttered those rolls—I was building something. I was showing up in love. I was creating a safe place not just for Tim, but for myself too. A place where I could taste what it felt like to be needed again—not for who I used to be, but for who I was becoming.

Sometimes, I'd go the extra mile—not out of obligation, but out of a quiet joy that was blooming in my chest. I'd put a sprig of rosemary on top of the mashed potatoes. I'd fold the napkin just a little nicer. I'd

CHAPTER 10

slice the pie so it looked like something out of a magazine, even if it was just Tim and me sitting at our little table in our small home.

Those were my love notes.

Not written in ink. Not sealed in envelopes. But tucked into casseroles and baked into cookies and whispered into warm mugs of coffee. When you've lived through something that tried to break you, finding gentle ways to love again becomes an act of courage. And for me, food was that brave little bridge.

Tim didn't always see the extra effort. He didn't always comment on the way I had browned the butter just right or dusted the edges of the pie with cinnamon. But that didn't matter. Because I saw it. I knew what I was doing. I was putting pieces of myself back together through those meals.

It reminded me of those early days of motherhood, when my babies were small and the world outside felt too big. Back then, too, I cooked with love tucked into every spoonful. I'd cut sandwiches into shapes. I'd make pancakes that looked like hearts. I'd serve macaroni with a sprinkle of parsley and say, "Fancy restaurant," just to see them smile.

That instinct—to feed people with tenderness—never left me. Even after the dark years. Even after the weight gain. Even after the fear settled deep in my bones.

There were seasons when I didn't recognize myself in the mirror. When the trauma showed itself in the way I carried extra pounds, in the way I avoided eye contact, in the way I shrunk from attention. But in the kitchen? I always knew who I was.

A woman who pours love into food.

A woman who turns grief into gravy.

A woman who stirs healing into soup.

It may sound simple, but it's not. It's holy work. Quiet, sacred, unseen work. It's a prayer whispered into a pot of stew. A hope folded into warm biscuit dough. A promise that says, "I'm still here. And I'm still loving."

When I feed Tim, I'm not just nourishing his body—I'm showing him that I care, that I choose him, that his presence at our table matters. And when he thanks me, when he leans back with a satisfied sigh and says, "That was *so* good," I feel something rise up in me. Not pride, exactly. More like *peace*. Like maybe, in that moment, everything is okay.

There's a sacred rhythm in setting the table. In lighting a candle. In pouring a drink. In asking, "Would you like seconds?" There's beauty in cleaning the counters, in wrapping up leftovers, in packing lunch for the next day. These are the things that carry me forward. These are the quiet rituals that hold my days together.

I don't always get it right. Some nights I'm too tired to cook. Some nights I order takeout or throw together something simple and messy and imperfect. But even then, there's grace. Because love doesn't need to be polished to be real. It just needs to be present.

That's what I'm learning over and over.

That home isn't found in the fancy or the flawless.

It's found in the ordinary. In the imperfect. In the trying.

It's found in a kitchen that smells like cinnamon and garlic. In a woman who has been through the fire and still chooses to create something warm for someone she loves. In a home that might not be perfect but is full of heart.

And maybe, just maybe, that's the kind of worship God loves best.

Not the loud kind. Not the big showy kind.

But the quiet offering of a life lived with intention.

A table set with love.

A heart poured into pie crust.

A routine that becomes a refuge.

A woman who finds the holy in the ordinary.

And learns—slowly, gently—to see herself as sacred too.

Chapter 11

Before Tim ever knocked on the door of my life, there was a moment when I didn't know if I'd survive at all.

Three months before he came, I was being held prisoner in my own home—but not by a stranger. By my own son. My oldest boy. The one I carried. The one I raised. The one I fought so hard to protect. Somewhere along the line, he'd decided I was no longer fit to exist outside the walls of a locked room. And I don't say that with drama. I say it because it's the truth.

He had become my legal guardian without my knowledge—paperwork filed quietly, behind my back. While I was still trying to find my footing through layers of trauma, medication changes, and depression, he had already made up his mind: I needed to be put away. Permanently.

He was angry—always angry in those days. Slamming doors. Punching holes in the walls. Snapping over nothing. The fear in my chest wasn't just emotional—it was physical. It lived in my bones. It followed me from room to room. But eventually, I wasn't even allowed to move from room to room anymore. I was kept in my bedroom like a ghost. The rest of the house wasn't mine anymore.

I was locked away, hidden, hushed.

Two weeks. I stayed in that room for two solid weeks, too scared to push back, too afraid of what he might do. I wasn't allowed to eat with him. Wasn't allowed to leave the room without tension so thick it strangled. I slept with my back to the wall, shaking with a fear that was all too familiar. Different man. Different betrayal. Same helplessness.

But God, somehow, there's always a thread—even in the worst of it.

One afternoon, with the light barely reaching through the blinds, I found a cell phone shoved deep in the bottom drawer of my nightstand. I don't even remember putting it there. But there it was. And when I held the button down, the screen lit up—1% battery.

One percent.

I didn't even think. My fingers just moved. I dialed my brother's number and whispered one word: *Help*. Then the phone went dark in my hand.

It felt like the longest two hours of my life.

And then... a crash. Wood splintering. My bedroom door giving way to my brother, busting through like a rescue team. And behind him, the police.

I was stunned. Frozen. My son was yelling. My brother was demanding to get inside. The police stood between it all like referees in a game where nobody was playing fair.

They gave me ten minutes.

Ten minutes to grab what I could, get out, and figure it out from there. I'll never forget the way I looked around my bedroom—the last space I'd been allowed to call mine—and felt this wave of both devastation and relief. I was leaving. I didn't know where I was going. But I was finally walking out.

Before I left, I turned to my son—this child I had once rocked in my arms—and I said something I meant with every ounce of myself: "Everything better be here when I come back to get the rest of my things."

But when I returned a few weeks later, he was gone.

And so was everything else.

The house was stripped bare.

CHAPTER 11

Furniture, dishes, photos... gone. It didn't even feel like a home anymore. It was just a shell. And maybe, in some twisted way, that matched how I felt inside.

I had to stay with my mom after that. There wasn't anywhere else to go. She let me in, yes—but not without conditions. Not without coldness. Not without judgment. She didn't offer comfort. She didn't ask what happened. She didn't want to hear the truth. She just gave me a place to sleep... and her silence.

I stayed for a month. I kept my head down. I tried not to breathe too loudly. Tried not to exist too fully. And all the while, my heart broke over and over. Over what my son did. Over how little my mother seemed to care. Over the fact that I had nowhere to land and no one to trust.

But then... Tim came.

And everything changed.

* * *

There's a heaviness that comes from being unloved by the one person who's supposed to love you no matter what. A weight that settles into your bones and never quite lets up, even on the good days. You carry it like luggage you didn't pack—but somehow, you've been dragging it with you for as long as you can remember.

That was my mother.

She didn't hit me. She didn't scream at me daily. But her weapon of choice was more subtle. More dangerous in a way. It was silence. It was neglect. It was absence. It was the way she turned her face away from the ugliest things that happened to me and pretended they weren't there.

She knew what that man did to me when I was a little girl. She knew what happened the night he came into my room and touched me under my nightgown—made me put my hand on him in ways a child never should. She knew. I told her. And she let him stay anyway. That's the kind of betrayal that breaks something in you forever.

He stayed in the house for months after. Ate at the same table as me. Walked down the same hallway. Smiled at me like he hadn't stolen something sacred. I used to pray at night, not for safety—but to be invisible. If I could just disappear, maybe the hurt would too.

And my mother? She barely blinked. She didn't ask if I was okay. She didn't scream at him. She didn't throw him out. She didn't hold me and cry and say, "I'm sorry this happened to you." She didn't choose me.

That was the beginning of the unraveling between us. But I didn't cut her off. I was too desperate. I still wanted her to love me. I still wanted her to show up. I spent decades chasing the crumbs of her affection, accepting the bare minimum and calling it "family."

Even as an adult, I bent myself into pieces to earn a seat at her table. I loaned money I couldn't afford to lose. I drove her places. I bought her gifts. I forgave her silences. I looked past the jabs she made about my weight, my home, my choices. I let her treat Tim like he was trash under her shoe—polite in public, cold behind closed doors.

I kept showing up.

Because deep down, there's this aching hope in every daughter that someday, somehow, her mother will finally see her.

But mine never did.

When I brought Tim into my life, I finally had someone who stood beside me without conditions. Someone who didn't demand perfection. Someone who didn't shame me for my past or use my trauma against me. Tim was quiet, gentle, steady. And I think that scared her. Because Tim made it harder for her to control me. Tim gave me a mirror that reflected love, not shame. And that didn't sit well.

From the beginning, she dismissed him. Said he was just "using" me. Said he wasn't good enough. Never gave him a chance. Not once. And worse, she tried to poison my kids against him too. The oldest ones listened. They believed her stories. They clung to her side like soldiers in a war I never declared.

I kept hoping she'd come around. That maybe time would soften her. That maybe seeing how happy I was, how stable, how at peace I felt in this quiet little life Tim and I were building—maybe that would melt her coldness.

But it didn't.

Instead, she doubled down. Became meaner. Harsher. She'd say things like, "You're always choosing him over your family," as if she hadn't made me choose a thousand times before—between her approval and my own sanity. Between being the daughter she wanted and being the woman I actually am.

As the years passed and she got older, it only got worse. She became cruel in ways that didn't even feel like passive-aggression anymore. It was just aggression. Plain and unapologetic. She'd call and leave nasty voicemails. She'd complain to other family members about me—painting me as ungrateful, selfish, dramatic. She'd dig up the ugliest parts of my past just to throw them at my feet again.

And I let it continue for too long. I kept trying. Kept answering the phone. Kept visiting, even when it left me shaking. Kept explaining Tim to her. Kept explaining *me* to her.

But no matter what I did, she always made me feel like a burden. Like I was never enough.

And one day... I just couldn't do it anymore.

I remember the day clearly. I was standing at my kitchen sink—my safe place, my sanctuary—and she had just hung up on me after one of her usual verbal lashings. No apology. No softness. Just more guilt, more venom. And I stood there, my hands in soapy water, and I thought, *Why am I doing this to myself?*

Why was I letting her voice drown out all the healing I'd worked so hard for?

Why was I letting her presence steal the peace I'd finally found?

Why was I still waiting for her to become someone she never wanted to be?

I turned off the water. Dried my hands. Sat down at the table. And I said, out loud—maybe to God, maybe to myself, maybe to the little girl inside me who never got the mother she deserved—"It's time."

And that was it.

There was no big blowout. No final confrontation. No letter sent or phone thrown or Facebook rant. I just… stopped.

I stopped calling. Stopped answering. Stopped justifying. Stopped defending Tim. Stopped begging for her to love me.

I let go.

And I cried. Oh, I cried. Because letting go of a mother, even a toxic one, feels like cutting off a limb. It feels like betrayal, even when you know it's survival. It feels like death, even when it's the beginning of life.

But the peace that followed?

It was like stepping into sunlight after years underground.

I could breathe. I could laugh without the tightness in my chest. I could share photos of Tim without bracing for her disapproval. I could enjoy my mornings without waiting for a phone call that would ruin my day. I could choose myself without guilt.

And Tim? He never said, "I told you so." He just held me. Quietly. Fully. Like someone who had been waiting for me to come home to myself.

He made me a cup of tea that night. Rubbed my back. Sat beside me on the couch while I let the grief come. And in his presence, I finally understood what a safe love feels like. A love that doesn't demand you shrink. A love that doesn't punish you for protecting your peace. A love that says, "I'm here. And you're not crazy for walking away."

Because I wasn't crazy.

CHAPTER 11

I was just done.

Done with being last. Done with being used. Done with being the scapegoat in someone else's story. Done with begging to be seen.

I was done.

And you know what?

It's been nearly a year since I made that choice. Since I walked away and chose myself. And not once have I regretted it. Not once have I wished I could go back. Because what I gained was worth far more than what I lost.

I gained silence where there used to be chaos.

I gained self-respect where there used to be shame.

I gained love—real love—with a man who sees me, hears me, supports me.

I gained myself.

That's the truth nobody tells you about letting go: It hurts. It shatters. It leaves scars. But it also sets you free. It clears the air. It makes room for better.

Sometimes healing requires subtraction.

Sometimes love begins with saying, "No more."

And letting go of my mother?

It wasn't an act of hate.

It was the deepest, most radical act of love I'd ever given to myself.

* * *

There's a strange kind of grief that comes when you lose something that was never fully yours—but felt like it should have been.

For years, my mom had told me that her house—the home she and my stepdad shared for over two decades—would one day be mine. It was in her will. She said it clearly, more than once, that when the time came, she would gift it to me. And I believed her. Not because

I expected anything, not because I was waiting with hands outstretched, but because that house... it held pieces of my life.

It held memories of my stepdad, the man who raised me through my teenage years. I could still picture him in his recliner, still hear his laughter echo through the living room on holidays. It was the house where my children, when they were little, used to run barefoot across the kitchen floor, giggling. Where birthdays were celebrated. Where Christmas trees stood in the corner year after year, wrapped in the same ornaments and tangled lights.

It wasn't just a house. It was history. It was roots. And even though my mom and I had a complicated, painful relationship, I guess a part of me still hoped that maybe—just maybe—some thread of love or legacy would stay unbroken. That I would at least be remembered in a way that felt... kind.

But instead, she called me one day and said, almost casually, that she was putting the house up for sale.

No heads-up. No warmth. No kindness behind it.

She said, "You'd probably just sell it anyway."

Like I was careless. Like I didn't understand what it meant. Like I hadn't held that home in my heart for all these years.

It hit me like a slap.

And then she said something that stung even deeper.

She told me my brother and his wife, Cindy, were helping her make all the decisions now. That they were the ones helping her move closer to them—an hour and a half away from me. She said she had asked Cindy whether she should call and tell me ahead of time, and Cindy told her not to. Said to wait. Said to have everything in place first.

And my mom listened.

They planned it all without me. She packed up, made arrangements, moved out—and never said goodbye.

I didn't even know she had left until I happened to drive by the old

CHAPTER 11

place a few weeks later and saw the *For Sale* sign hanging in the window. It was just... there. No call. No message. No explanation. Just a sign that told me everything: you weren't included. You're not part of this anymore.

It felt like grief stacked on top of grief. I had already lost her emotionally, over and over again through the years. Her coldness. Her passive-aggressive comments. Her tendency to treat me like I was less. But this? This was a final kind of goodbye—a decision to erase me from the picture altogether.

She didn't just sell a house. She sold our history.

And I wasn't even worth a phone call.

She said Cindy was "smarter than me." That's why she put her second in command after my brother for medical decisions and her estate. Said it as if I was too dumb to be trusted with her well-being. And maybe she thought I'd be too emotional. Maybe she thought I wouldn't follow orders the way she wanted. But all I heard was: *You're not enough.* Again.

It brought me back to being a child. Sitting at the dinner table, waiting for approval. Wanting to be noticed. Wanting to be loved in the way that wasn't conditional or laced with sarcasm. Wanting to feel chosen, just once.

But she never did choose me. Not really. And this—this final decision—made that fact louder than ever.

It's hard to put into words what it feels like to lose your mother over and over again, in new ways, even as an adult. It doesn't matter how old you get, that longing to be seen never fully goes away. And when it's denied over and over, it doesn't just hurt—it reshapes you.

That house, with its red front door and the creaky step by the back patio, used to be a place that smelled like turkey on Thanksgiving and summer watermelon. Now it's just a reminder. A symbol of what I wasn't given. Of the memories she moved away from without even blinking.

Tim held me that day. When I came home after driving past the house, I walked in the door and didn't even take off my shoes. I just crumbled into his arms and cried.

"She never called," I kept saying. "She never even said goodbye." And Tim, in his steady way, didn't try to fix it. He just held me. Let me fall apart for a while. Let me mourn, not just the house, but the fantasy I had held onto for so long—that one day, somehow, she'd see my worth.

That moment—sobbing into his shoulder, shaking with a grief so old and so fresh all at once—that was when I really let her go.

Not out of anger. Not out of bitterness.

Out of self-preservation.

Out of the realization that I cannot keep handing over pieces of myself to someone who will never handle them with care.

And since that day, I've started building a different kind of life. One that doesn't orbit around whether or not my mother accepts me. One that isn't held hostage by the hope that maybe she'll change.

She won't. And I'm no longer sacrificing my peace on the altar of her approval.

Instead, I've created a home with Tim where kindness is the default. Where quiet mornings are spent in our tiny kitchen sipping coffee and talking about what we're grateful for. Where I decorate with things I love and cook food that smells like comfort. Where no one tells me I'm too emotional or too sensitive. Where my love is received without conditions.

I still drive past the old house sometimes. Not on purpose, but by habit. And every time I do, it hurts a little less. I still feel the ache, like a bruise being pressed, but it doesn't break me open anymore. I look at that *For Sale* sign and I think: *Let it go. Let someone else build something new there.*

Because now, I'm building something new right here.

A life that feels soft.

CHAPTER 11

A love that feels safe.

A peace that wasn't handed to me—I had to fight for it.

But it's mine now. And I will protect it.

I may not have inherited her home. But I am reclaiming something far more sacred:

Myself.

Chapter 12

Peace isn't what I thought it would be.

I used to imagine peace as some grand thing—soft music playing, sunlight streaming through lace curtains, everything neat and quiet and serene, like a magazine photo you'd rip out and tape on your dream board. But the real peace? The kind I've been learning to live with these last few years? It's heavier than I expected. Heavier and quieter and a little bit wild in the way it surprises me on ordinary days.

It crept in, not with a parade, but like warm air seeping under the door of a cold room.

It looked like mismatched coffee mugs drying by the sink. It smelled like bread baking on a day when I didn't feel like talking. It sounded like the tv in the living room while Tim relaxed in the recliner chair. It felt like breathing—really breathing—for the first time after years of holding my breath.

Peace is built slowly. It's not bought at once or gifted by anyone else. It's earned through days and days of choosing something different. Choosing quiet instead of conflict. Choosing presence instead of panic. Choosing love that stays instead of fear that haunts. It's a home where the loudest sound is the purr of the cat or the hum of the oven.

And maybe most of all—it's knowing I don't have to prove anything to anyone in my own home.

That truth right there took me a long time to accept. After everything

CHAPTER 12

I'd been through—the trauma, the weight gain, the abandonment, the unraveling of relationships with people who should've stayed—I got used to always being on edge. Always explaining. Always watching. But slowly, in this small home with Tim, something started to shift.

It wasn't one big moment.

It was quiet things.

The way Tim folds his clothes and lays them gently on the dresser like someone who's never known what it means to rush. The way we play checkers in the evenings and laugh when Tim wins every single time. The way we both like the house dim in the early evening, with just the lamp glowing next to the couch. There's nothing flashy here. Nothing grand. But every corner of this place holds the comfort of being known.

I didn't know how much I needed that until I had it.

And I think sometimes, when you've lived through as much noise as I have—screaming, breaking, chaos—you don't even realize you're addicted to the sound of survival. Silence used to scare me. I'd fill it with TV, music, chores, anything to keep from being left alone with my thoughts. But now, I welcome the hush. I crave it.

I let it wash over me while I'm stirring soup or wiping down the counter. I let it settle into the room while I read beside Tim at night, both of us lost in our own pages, our own thoughts, but still right there beside one another. That's a kind of peace I didn't even know how to pray for years ago.

Our home isn't fancy. We live simply. A trailer tucked between trees with a cozy kitchen, a little dining nook, and a living room that always smells like whatever candle I've lit that day—vanilla, cinnamon apple, sometimes something floral if I'm in the mood to pretend it's spring again. The furniture isn't matching, but it's ours. The floors aren't new, but they hold the weight of love and healing now. They've held my feet on the days I cried. They've held Tim's when he danced with me slow to music no one else could hear.

This home holds all of that.

And it didn't come easy. It came after loss. After people walked out. After I let go of the hope that they'd ever walk back in.

My kids, I love them more than anything. But it's not what I dreamed it would be. Two of them are gone from my life. The other two—well, they drift in and out, showing up when they can, when they're ready. I don't chase them like I used to. I still love them, still hope for more, but I stopped begging to be seen.

And my mama... well, you know that story. I had to let her go. Let go of the hope that she'd ever say, "You matter to me." Let go of the idea that one day she'd show up with something soft in her tone or an apology in her eyes. She didn't. She won't. And driving past that house she left behind still tugs at something deep in me—but I don't break like I used to. I don't shatter.

Because here's the thing: my home now isn't filled with the noise of absence.

It's filled with the presence of peace.

It's filled with a man who shows up every day and loves me without conditions. Who takes out the trash, and warms up my coffee, and holds me when I wake from a nightmare. Who sees me—in all my mess, in all my quiet sadness, in all my soft, weary strength—and stays anyway.

Peace is him sitting at the table while I make dinner. Not offering to help, not hovering—just there. Just present. Just content to exist in the same space as me, without needing me to perform or pretend.

Peace is the way we do things without speaking sometimes. The rhythm we've built. I put the towels in the wash, he takes them out. I start the stew, he gets the bowls. I light the candle, he dims the lights. It's a dance we've learned together. And it's soft. So soft.

Sometimes I sit in the quiet of the morning, before the day really begins, and I just breathe. The house is still, the cats are stretched out in little warm circles, and the light is low. I make my tea, stir it slow,

CHAPTER 12

and I let my mind wander—but not too far. I let myself feel the weight of peace.

Because it is a weight. It's not empty. It's not airy. It's grounded. Heavy in a good way. Like a warm quilt across your chest on a cold night. Like the hush of snow outside while soup simmers on the stove. It's not loud, but it has presence. It fills the room.

And it fills me.

I'm still learning how to hold it. How to let it in and let it stay. I still catch myself waiting for the other shoe to drop sometimes. Still flinch at kindness. Still struggle to believe that maybe, just maybe, I'm allowed to rest.

But this home, these quiet things—it's teaching me.

It's teaching me that I don't have to earn peace. That I don't have to explain it. That I can simply dwell in it. That maybe healing doesn't look like what I thought. Maybe it looks like soup bubbling on the stove while the man I love reaches into the cupboard for the bowls without asking where they are.

Maybe it looks like silence that doesn't feel like loneliness.

Maybe it looks like cinnamon in the air and soft light on the table and knowing that no one here is going to hurt me.

This chapter of my life isn't loud. It's not full of applause or recognition. But it's rich. Rich in the kind of way that doesn't show up on the outside but fills me from within.

A home built of quiet things... it saved me.

Not because it was perfect.

But because it was *safe*.

And after everything, that is more than enough.

* * *

You wouldn't think much of it, our little home from the outside. It's just a single-wide trailer tucked behind a patch of overgrown rose bushes and a gravel drive that crunches when Tim pulls in from work. But inside? Inside, it's a soft place to land.

And I don't just mean soft because of the throw blankets or the quilt on the back of the loveseat or the worn chair Tim sinks into every evening like it's the only place in the world meant for him. I mean *soft* in that soul-deep way. The kind of soft that holds you when life's been too hard for too long. The kind of soft that feels like exhaling after years of holding your breath.

It's quiet here. Most days, the loudest thing is the washer humming in the background or the click of Tim's spoon against his coffee cup. And I've come to love that stillness. In a life that's been flooded with sirens, screaming, slammed doors, and nights spent curled up in fear—I've learned that stillness isn't scary anymore. It's sacred.

That stillness is what allows me to *feel* now. Not just survive. Not just get through. But to actually *be*—with my thoughts, with my emotions, with the kind of quiet that doesn't demand anything from me. It just lets me exist.

It took me a long time to understand that.

For a while, even after Tim moved in and life had settled down, I still moved like a woman ready to run. I'd clean the house frantically for no reason. I'd check the locks two, three, four times before bed. I'd have one foot always dangling over the edge of safety, waiting for the next thing to go wrong. Because that's what life had taught me—if things were too calm, too good, too easy, it probably meant something awful was around the corner.

But Tim? He never pushed me to relax. Never told me I was being "too much" or "too anxious." He just stayed. Sat with me while I stared at the wall, made me coffee when I hadn't spoken a word all morning, offered his hand without expecting me to take it.

He waited.

CHAPTER 12

That was the greatest act of love I've ever been given—someone willing to wait while I learned how to breathe.

Over time, I started leaning into the slowness. The routines. The safe predictability of our days. It didn't happen all at once, but little by little, our life became a rhythm I didn't want to escape.

Like how every morning, I wake before him—not because I *have* to, but because I *want* to. The house is still dark, the cats are usually tangled at the end of the bed, and I tiptoe out to the kitchen with my slippers and that robe I can't seem to part with, even though the sleeves are fraying.

The kettle goes on. The candle gets lit. It's nothing fancy—just my quiet way of greeting the day. I sit at the table, hands wrapped around my mug, steam rising in little curls like a blessing, and I think about nothing in particular. Sometimes I pray. Sometimes I just watch the sky shift from black to purple to that soft, early gray.

Tim usually wakes to the smell of fresh brewed coffee, and he shuffles in with sleepy eyes and a crooked smile that still makes my heart skip like it did twelve years ago. We don't talk much at first. We don't need to. There's something tender about those quiet mornings—the kind of love that doesn't need grand gestures to be felt.

And later, when the day unfolds with its usual pace, I settle into the rhythm I've come to love.

Making the bed. Opening the blinds. Lighting a new candle for the day. A little tidy here, a little laundry there. Sometimes I turn on music. Sometimes I just let the house breathe.

Tim goes about his routine—tools and projects, fixing this or that, talking to himself in that endearing way he does when something isn't working quite right. We move around each other like two puzzle pieces that finally figured out how to fit—not perfect, but placed just right.

And that's the beauty of this life now. I don't feel like I have to earn it. I'm not constantly fighting to prove I'm worthy of being loved or safe or allowed to just *be*. I'm not waiting for the other shoe to drop.

I'm barefoot in the kitchen, flipping through recipes, not because I'm filming a video or writing them down for anyone else—but because I *want* to make something warm for the man who loves me.

There's something deeply healing about doing that.

Cooking for Tim isn't a chore. It's an offering. A quiet way of saying, "I still choose you." And he sees it—every casserole, every biscuit, every pot of homemade stew. He thanks me every time. And not in that obligatory way. In that soft-spoken, sincere, I-know-what-you-put-into-this way. It means more than I can say.

Evenings are where the rhythm settles even deeper. Tim in his chair, me on the loveseat with a blanket across my lap and a book I may or may not actually read. Sometimes we watch something together. Sometimes we sit in silence. There are nights where I reach across to hold his hand without a word, and he just squeezes back, like, "I know." And he does.

This peace we've built—it's not loud. It's not perfect. It's not what anyone from the outside might call glamorous. But it's *ours*. It's steady. It's rooted. It's been watered with time and patience and grace.

I used to crave excitement. Maybe because chaos was the only thing that ever made me feel alive. But now, I crave softness. I crave these evenings. These quiet meals. These routines that make the world feel less scary.

And it's not because everything is easy now. It's not. There are still hard days. There are still wounds that sting, memories that come rushing in when I least expect them. I still struggle with my reflection some mornings. Still catch myself wanting to shrink back into invisibility. But the difference is—I don't do it alone anymore.

When the weight of the world feels too much, I have someone beside me who notices. Who says, "Let's go for a drive." Who puts the kettle on. Who rubs my back while I cry, even if I can't explain why the tears came in the first place.

CHAPTER 12

This is what peace looks like now.

It's not loud or flashy or boastful.

It's the way Tim knows exactly how I like my tea. It's the way the curtains flutter in the evening breeze. It's the smell of garlic and rosemary on a Tuesday night. It's the way our house settles with the dusk, and I find myself breathing deeper without even realizing it.

It's the stillness I used to fear, now becoming the safest place I know.

It's the gift of no longer walking on eggshells.

It's the miracle of not being afraid of bedtime.

It's the freedom to wake up in the morning and not brace for a fight.

This house, this love, this quiet—it's all made of little, ordinary things. But each one is stitched with threads of something beautiful. Something that says, "You've made it. And you're still making it. One day at a time."

I think often of how far I've come. Not in that self-congratulatory way. But in the way someone who's been to the bottom of the pit realizes she's not in the dark anymore. I don't measure success by how much I've accomplished. I measure it by how safe I feel in my own skin.

And that... that took years.

But now, with Tim by my side, with the routines that hold me and the softness of a home I helped shape—I finally have a soft place to land.

And that changes everything.

∗ ∗ ∗

There was a time when every sound was something to fear. Every footstep outside my door, every creak in the floor, every unexpected noise after sunset—it all sent a ripple of panic through my body. I lived in that heightened state for so long that I forgot what silence could feel like when it wasn't the pause before something bad happened.

But now? Now, the house makes a different kind of music.

It's taken me years to notice it. Years of healing. Years of creating this little world inside these walls where peace has room to stretch out and settle. And now, the very sounds that once made me flinch... they comfort me. They tell me I'm home.

The floor creaks every time Tim walks down the hallway in the morning. It's the same spot—just outside the bathroom—and it used to startle me. But now, I hear it and smile. That sound means he's up. That the day is beginning like any other. That he's going to come into the kitchen with that sleepy voice and say, "Mornin', babylove," like he always does.

It's the sound of routine. Of normal. Of safe.

The wind knocks against our windows sometimes. This trailer's old, and nothing seals quite like it used to. So when a strong gust comes through, the pane by the loveseat rattles just a little. And years ago, that would've sent me to my feet in a panic—checking locks, looking through curtains, heart pounding. But now? Now I just glance up from my book or the dough I'm kneading, and I say, "Sounds like the wind's picking up." And that's it.

Because I'm not bracing for danger anymore. I'm just listening to the weather roll through.

It's funny how your body can relearn things. How it can unlearn fear, little by little. How the nervous system—so wired for survival—can start to trust again. It doesn't happen overnight. But it does happen.

I know that now.

And it's not just the house. It's Tim too. The way he moves through our space. I used to jump every time someone came up behind me. Even if they weren't loud. Even if they didn't mean harm. It didn't matter. My body still remembered other times—times when footsteps meant danger. When someone standing too close meant I wasn't safe.

CHAPTER 12

But Tim learned me. That's what I always say. He didn't just learn about me. He *learned* me. The way I moved. The way I flinched. The way I'd stiffen if someone stood too close without warning.

So now, when he comes up behind me in the kitchen, he says something first. "I'm just grabbing a plate." "Just me, sweetheart." Just enough to let me know it's him. And even though I don't flinch anymore, he still does it. Not because he has to—but because he's kind. Because he wants this home to always be a place where I feel held. Seen. Safe.

Even the door shutting—something so small—feels different now.

Before, that sound would've made my whole body go tense. A door closing meant someone entering. Someone leaving. Something changing. I never knew if it was something I should be afraid of.

Now? It's just Tim running out to grab something from the truck. It's the sound of a package being delivered. It's the screen door clicking shut after I sweep of the front porch.

Nothing more. Nothing less. Just the normal sounds of a life.

I never thought I'd get here. Not really. Not to a place where a door doesn't send me spiraling. Where the fridge humming doesn't make me hyper-aware of every other sound in the house. Where silence isn't deafening.

And that's the thing—I used to be so afraid of silence.

It wasn't peaceful to me. It was dangerous. It meant something was coming. It meant something had happened. It meant I needed to prepare. I kept TVs on. Radios humming. Anything to fill the air.

But now?

Now I crave the quiet.

I sit in it like it's a warm bath. Like it's something earned. And maybe it is.

In the mornings, when Tim's gone and the house is mine alone, I listen to the soft things—the click of the stove, the gurgle of the coffee pot, the gentle scrape of my slippered feet on the linoleum. I hear the birds outside, the way the wind brushes through the old trees, the faint hum of the dryer tumbling our clothes. I hear the steady, gentle rhythm of a house lived in with care.

It's not silent. But it's not loud either. It's just *soft*. And after a life that's been so sharp, so loud, so jarring—that softness is a kind of salvation.

Even the sound of my own breath feels different now.

There were years when I couldn't even *hear* it. When I was holding it so often I didn't realize I was doing it. When I lived in a constant state of tension so thick it was like my lungs forgot how to work right.

But now? Now I can sit on the couch with a blanket, look around our little living room, and take a deep breath *all the way in*. All the way out. And I can hear it. Feel it. Be *grateful* for it.

The sound of safe isn't just about what you hear.

It's about what you don't hear anymore.

It's not hearing screaming through the walls.

It's not hearing sirens outside your door.

It's not hearing your own heartbeat in your ears every time you step into a dark room.

It's the absence of those things that creates a new kind of soundtrack. One made up of soft pans clinking in the sink. The creak of the recliner. The rustle of the leaves against the kitchen window. The gentle *thunk* of a book being closed.

There are days when I think back to the version of myself who didn't think this kind of peace was possible. Who thought she would always live half-in, half-out of her life. Who thought healing was only for other people, braver people, stronger people.

But I was wrong.

Because healing looks like this.

It looks like falling asleep to the sound of rain and not waking in a

CHAPTER 12

panic.

It looks like listening to Tim's quiet breathing beside me and feeling safe enough to close my eyes again.

It looks like frying onions in a pan while a record plays in the background, knowing no one's coming through the door to hurt me.

It looks like sitting in the quiet, letting the stillness be enough.

I used to think sound was the enemy. Now I know it was never the sound—it was the association. The trauma. The memory. And I've spent the last few years building new ones.

Now, when I hear the oven beep, I don't brace—I smile. It means dinner's ready. It means something I made is about to be shared.

When I hear Tim laugh from the other room, I don't flinch—I soften. It means there's joy here. It means he's still with me. It means we've built something worth keeping.

When I hear the wind howling at the windows, I don't panic—I grab a blanket. It means we're warm and safe inside. It means I don't have to run.

The sound of safe is ordinary.

But it is everything.

It's the way Tim says "I love you" at random times, just because.

It's the way the coffee brews at the same time every morning.

It's the way the cat jumps onto the bed, purring like a tiny motor, reminding me that life still vibrates with small, sweet things.

It's the sound of healing, unfolding in real time.

Not with fanfare.

Not with applause.

But with the simple music of two people making a life together.

Quiet.

Steady.

True.

And now, when I sit in the stillness of our home—blanket over my lap, warm drink in hand, Tim humming to himself in the next room—I don't feel afraid of what's next.

I feel ready.

Because I've come to understand something I didn't know before: peace isn't the absence of sound.

Peace is knowing which sounds mean you're safe.

Chapter 13

There's this strange stillness that drifts in after the holidays, and I never quite know what to do with it. The tree is down. The candles that glowed in every window have been tucked back into their boxes. The cinnamon-scented pinecones are tossed, the garland's gone brittle, and suddenly... it's just me and Tim again, sitting in the quiet, trying to remember what ordinary life felt like before all the sparkle.

And I love Christmas—I always have. The lights, the cooking, the soft music, the little moments of giving, the chance to make things feel just a little more magical. But once it's over, once the decorations are packed away and the leftovers are gone, there's this hush that settles over everything. The house feels a little too still, like it's exhaling from all the festivity. And sometimes, I find myself holding my breath too, wondering what to do with all that stillness.

Because it's just us. Me and Tim.

The kids are grown now. They have their own lives, their own homes, their own holiday tables to gather around. And while I know that's how it's supposed to be—how it's meant to go—it doesn't stop the ache. I still remember what it used to be like. The chaos, the laughter, the paper flying across the living room, the sound of little feet running down the hallway to see if Santa came. Now, it's just a quiet morning and a cup of coffee for two.

And still, I try to make it special. I bake the pies. I set the table. I light the candles. I hum along with the same carols I've played for decades. I even wrap a few gifts in tissue paper and bows, even though we've long since stopped doing big presents. It's not about the gifts—it never was. It's about making the moment feel like something. It's about giving the memory of Christmas a place to sit down and stay awhile.

But once it's over—once the last cookie is eaten and the final candle has burned low—I always find myself in that strange, quiet place. The days between Christmas and the New Year feel slow and slippery, like water running through your fingers. And once the new year begins, there's an emptiness I don't like to admit to. A kind of emotional hangover. The world moves on, the stores clear the shelves, the commercials shift to gym memberships and storage bins. And here I am, sitting in my little home, surrounded by the leftovers of joy, wondering if it's okay that I miss what was.

The house feels different after the holidays. Not bad, not sad exactly—just quieter. I'll be sitting on the couch with a blanket over my lap, the twinkle lights gone, and I'll glance at Tim and feel this deep, quiet gratitude that he's still here. That we still have this life, even if it's quieter than it used to be. We don't need the chaos anymore, but sometimes I still miss it. I miss the noise, the mess, the little voices calling out, "Look what I got!" I miss the way it used to feel when the house was full.

Now, it's just me lighting one candle at the table. Just one plate of leftovers. Just one pair of slippers by the door. Me and Tim, side by side, sharing a piece of pie and holding hands while the clock ticks into January.

And that's the truth of it—this new season of life is softer. Smaller. It doesn't come with grand gestures or big celebrations. It comes in the form of leftover ham sandwiches and quiet walks in the snow. It comes in sitting on the couch watching old Christmas movies on New Year's

CHAPTER 13

Day, even though the tree's already gone and the lights are boxed up. It comes in looking across the room at the man who never left, the man who makes this house feel like home, no matter how quiet it gets.

This is the part of the year no one really talks about. The part after the magic. The part where you're left with the memories and the mess and the long, cold stretch of winter ahead. The part where you have to find your joy again in smaller things—like a hot mug of tea, or a kitchen that smells like molasses, or a candle flickering while the snow falls outside.

And you know what I've realized?

This quiet? It holds a kind of healing too.

It's where the ache lives, yes—but it's also where the peace slips in, unnoticed at first, like sunlight sneaking across the floor. It's where Tim puts on his flannel robe in the morning and I pour us both a cup of coffee and we sit in the silence, side by side, saying nothing—but feeling everything. It's where I pull out my favorite recipes again, not because anyone's coming over, but because I want the house to smell warm. I want to bake a little comfort back into the walls.

It's in the quiet that I remember who I am now. A woman who has survived a thousand heartbreaks. A woman who no longer needs a full house to feel full inside. A woman who knows how to make a moment matter, even if it's just a slow breakfast at the kitchen table with the man she loves.

The quiet between holidays is a strange kind of grief. But it's also a strange kind of grace. And maybe that's the lesson—maybe the slowing down isn't the end of the joy, but the beginning of a deeper one. One that doesn't need decorations or noise or a dozen people in the house. One that can be found in the soft clink of spoons in mugs and the way Tim's eyes crinkle when I bring him a plate of warm cornbread, just because.

This is our life now.

Not perfect. Not loud. But steady.
Just me and Tim.
And it's enough.

* * *

We don't do holidays like we used to.

There was a time, not all that long ago, when the days leading up to Thanksgiving and Christmas were loud and busy and packed full of trying to make everything perfect. Kids running through the house. Me running through my mind, trying to make sure the ham was thawed, the green beans had the crispy onions, the candles were lit, the napkins folded just so. I used to get caught up in trying to recreate some idea of a perfect holiday I saw in my head—a mix of Hallmark movies and old family memories, wrapped in cinnamon sticks and red ribbons.

But the truth is, that version of the holidays doesn't exist anymore.

The kids are grown and scattered. Some don't speak to me. Some drift in and out. And my mother—the woman who once carved the turkey while humming to herself—has been cut off completely. Not because I stopped loving her, but because love can't live where cruelty keeps setting the table. That choice still stings, especially during the holidays. But it also brought me peace I never thought I'd have.

Now? It's just me and Tim.

And at first, that quiet felt unbearable. Like a big, echoing house inside my heart. Too much silence. Too much space where memories used to live. But slowly—almost gently—we started making our own way. Our own traditions. Not the kind that demand perfection or leave you exhausted by the end of the day. No, these are soft, quiet, deeply personal. Traditions that don't care what the calendar says or whether anyone else shows up.

CHAPTER 13

Like cinnamon rolls on Christmas morning—not because anyone expects them, but because Tim smiles the moment he smells them baking. Like movie marathons with old favorites and fuzzy socks, no talking, just the kind of company that says everything without saying a word. Like drinking hot cocoa out of chipped mugs that only come out once a year, the kind that make us laugh because they're worn and faded and full of memories we've made *together*.

It's not always picture-perfect.

Sometimes, I light candles and cry through half of dinner because I'm remembering the way things used to be—the giggles, the toys scattered across the floor, the sound of my child saying "Mommy" like I was the most important person in the world. That ache? It never fully leaves. But I let it have its place at the table. I let it sit beside the mashed potatoes and the cranberry sauce and the rolls we bake together now, laughing when we forget to set the timer.

We don't do a giant tree anymore. Just a small one—three feet tall—that we put up in the corner of the living room. I string it with the same lights every year, and Tim always pretends not to notice when one bulb blinks out halfway through the season. We don't exchange piles of gifts. Maybe just a couple small things. Something useful. Something cozy. A new robe. A candle. A handwritten note.

And that's enough.

Sometimes it feels like we're creating a new language. One where "tradition" doesn't mean obligation or expectation—it means intimacy. It means choosing each other over and over again. It means asking, "What sounds good this year?" and really listening to the answer. It means letting go of what the holidays used to be and honoring what they are now.

We still make a big meal, though. Not because anyone's coming over, but because food is love in our house. And I still set the table. I still pull out the cloth napkins, even if they don't match. I still tuck a little sprig of pine into the centerpiece and play soft music in the background. Not for the photos. Not for the performance. Just for the feeling. Just for us.

One Thanksgiving, a couple years ago, I made the full spread—turkey, stuffing, candied yams, the works—and we sat there together in our quiet little home. No one else was there. No phones buzzing. No kids asking for second helpings. Just the two of us, a candle flickering, and the kind of silence that feels peaceful, not heavy.

Tim reached across the table and held my hand, and for a moment, it felt like the whole world stopped to exhale. He said, "This is the best meal I've ever had." And I believed him. Not because of the food, but because of the love that was in it. The effort. The softness. The healing.

That's what our holidays are now.

They're not about reclaiming what was lost. They're about cherishing what remains. About finding warmth in the quiet. About choosing joy, not chasing it. About laughing when the pie burns, and holding hands while the snow falls outside, and reminding ourselves that *this*—this slow, quiet, love-filled life—is still a gift.

We've learned how to make the ordinary feel sacred. A fire in the fireplace. A walk around the block on a snowy morning. A slow dance in the living room to some Willie Nelson song, with flour still on my apron and his arms wrapped around me like I'm the only thing in the world worth holding.

And maybe I am.

Maybe we both are.

Because this life? It hasn't been easy. We've both come from places that broke us down. We've both carried weight we never asked for. But here we are—two people who found each other, who built something real out of the ruins, who keep showing up for each other when the rest of the world goes quiet.

We may not have a house full of guests. We may not send out Christmas cards or bake a hundred cookies or hang lights across the

CHAPTER 13

whole roof. But we have *us*. We have warmth and kindness and understanding. We have tea in the evenings and soup on the stove. We have quiet mornings and candlelit dinners and the kind of love that doesn't need a season to be celebrated.

So yes, the holidays are different now.

But they're no less beautiful.

They've just grown up with us. Softened. Settled. Found their rhythm in the quiet. And I've learned, slowly, that just because the house isn't full doesn't mean my heart can't be. Just because the traditions have changed doesn't mean they've lost their meaning.

Because now, when I decorate the tree, I don't think about what I've lost.

I think about what I've kept.

And who's still here beside me.

And I say a quiet thank you for the man who holds my hand when the world feels too loud.

For the home we've built out of ordinary things.

For the life we've made—soft, simple, sacred.

Just the two of us.

* * *

There's a stillness to Christmas now that I never expected to love.

It's not the kind of stillness that comes from peace and snowflakes and soft choral music like the movies try to sell you. It's the kind of stillness that comes from loss, from distance, from letting go of what used to be—and then learning how to make that space your own. It's quiet. It's heavy sometimes. But it's also real. And for me and Tim, it's become something deeply sacred.

For years, the holidays felt like a spotlight shining down on everything I didn't have. Every empty chair. Every phone that didn't ring. Every unopened box of decorations I couldn't bring myself to pull out because it reminded me of a time when the house felt full, when laughter bounced off the walls and I was still trying to do everything right—for everyone.

But now? Christmas doesn't come with a to-do list. It doesn't come with pressure. It doesn't come with expectations I can't meet. It just… comes. Slowly. Softly. And somehow, that feels like a miracle in itself.

There are no stockings on the wall anymore. No big family dinner to plan. No noisy chaos of wrapping paper and kids running through the house in pajamas with sticky fingers. And honestly, that used to break my heart. It used to sit in my chest like a cold stone. I would ache for the noise. Ache for the mess. Ache for the chance to recreate something that had already slipped through my fingers.

But grief changes you. Time changes you.

And slowly, I started noticing something else: that the quiet wasn't empty. It was full. Full of little rituals, small comforts, gentle moments that wrapped themselves around me like a favorite blanket.

Now, Christmas starts for me the moment I light the first candle and take down the bin of decorations that sits quietly in the corner of our closet. There's not much in it—a few ornaments I've held onto over the years, a simple wreath, one string of warm white lights, and a tiny ceramic nativity that fits in the palm of my hand.

And Tim—he knows how much it means to me. He doesn't make a big show of helping, but he always finds a way to be nearby. He'll put on a pot of coffee or light a candle or turn on music—soft, slow, something instrumental with a little piano and maybe a violin—and let me move through it in my own rhythm.

I pull out each item with a kind of reverence. Not because they're fancy. They're not. But because they hold meaning. They carry stories. And they remind me that even though life looks different now, there is still beauty here. Still warmth. Still hope.

CHAPTER 13

The tree is small. We put it on a little table by the front window. Some years it's fake, pre-lit, and simple. Other years, if I'm feeling a little braver, I'll pick up a real one and let the smell of pine and winter settle into the house like a blessing. Either way, it's ours. And that's what makes it special.

We decorate it with old ornaments, some chipped, some glittering, some made by little hands that are now grown and far away. I don't match colors or themes anymore. I just hang what feels like home. A red wooden heart. A tiny baking whisk. A little glass gingerbread man with one leg missing. Each one whispers something soft to me when I hold it in my hands.

Sometimes I cry while decorating. Not out of sadness, really. Just out of feeling. Out of remembering. Out of letting it all pass through me like snow through the window—brief, quiet, and real. And Tim never asks me why. He just comes over, wraps his arms around me from behind, and lets me lean into him until the moment softens.

We wrap gifts for each other in brown paper and tie them with twine or ribbon I've had tucked in a drawer for years. Nothing expensive. Nothing big. Sometimes it's just a handwritten note. A jar of his favorite jam. A cozy pair of socks. One year, he had a old antique sled refurbished with a poem he wrote handwritten on it. Tears streamed down my cheeks as I read his loving words.

Christmas Eve is quiet. We turn off the lights except for the tree. We warm up something simple for dinner—maybe a bowl of stew, a loaf of crusty bread, a slice of pie. We eat at the table, across from each other, with candles lit and music playing low. We don't say much. We don't need to. The silence between us isn't uncomfortable anymore. It's warm. Familiar. Like a language we've both come to understand.

And after dinner, we sit on the couch with blankets and hot cocoa, and we talk about the year. Not in big dramatic ways. Just little reflections. "Remember when we planted the tomatoes too early?" or "That day we drove to the lake and got caught in the rain?" or "I loved that cinnamon roll recipe you tried in October." Small things. Quiet things. But they add up to a life.

Christmas morning, I still wake up early. Some habits never die. But now I don't rush. I let the light come in slowly through the curtains. I make a pot of coffee and heat up the cinnamon rolls I prepped the night before. I turn on the tree lights. I sit in my robe and fuzzy socks and wait for Tim to wake up.

When he comes into the room, sleepy-eyed and smiling, I always feel a little burst of joy. Not because it's Christmas. But because it's us. Still here. Still showing up for each other. Still making something out of all the quiet we were given.

We open our gifts slowly. One at a time. We savor it. We laugh. We sip coffee and let the morning stretch out like soft fabric across the floor. There's no schedule. No hurry. Just love, poured out in the way we look at each other. The way we say "thank you." The way we touch each other's hands and know—this is enough.

It took me years to believe that.

To believe that small could still be sacred. That quiet could still be full of life. That a Christmas with just two people could hold just as much magic as one with a house full of children and chaos and wrapping paper flying through the air.

But it does.

It's a new kind of Christmas. One built on healing. On choosing softness over performance. On honoring what was while embracing what is. It's not loud. It's not fancy. But it's warm. It's real. It's ours.

Sometimes, we drive through the neighborhoods to look at lights. We hold hands across the center console and point out our favorites. "Look at that snowman!" "Oh, I love that one—it's got the twinkly lights." "Can you imagine how long it took them to set all that up?" And we laugh. We wonder. We feel young again, just for a minute.

CHAPTER 13

When we get home, the house smells like pine and cinnamon and whatever was baking earlier that day. And we both breathe a little deeper. A little slower. Because home doesn't have to be filled with people to be filled with love.

And love—that's the real tradition now.

Not the kind that needs grand gestures or perfect photos.

But the kind that shows up in the simple things.

A clean kitchen. A warm cup of tea. A hand reaching for yours during a movie. A familiar song playing while the roast finishes in the oven.

Love that doesn't try to fix the past or control the future.

Love that lives in the now.

In the hush of snowfall.

In the flicker of candlelight.

In the way two people can sit together in silence and know that nothing is missing.

That this—this quiet, gentle, sacred holiday—is more than enough.

* * *

And I do love Christmas. I always have. I love the little rituals. The music, soft and nostalgic. The chance to make everything feel magical. The way one room, dressed in lights and warmth, can transform into something straight out of memory. I love the flour dusted across the counter. The smell of cinnamon and clove and fresh pine. The joy of giving, even when it's just small things, wrapped in paper and love.

But once it's over—when the tree is gone and the fridge holds only leftovers and the floor no longer carries the sound of visiting feet—there's a hush. A peculiar silence that settles over everything, like snow that fell after you'd already stopped watching. And in that hush, I find myself holding my breath, as though the quiet is too loud. As though, without the noise, I'll hear something I don't want to.

Because it's just us now.

Me and Tim.

The kids are grown. They have their own homes, their own routines, their own decorations tucked away in storage bins with labels in their handwriting. They're building their own magic, just like I once did when I was their age. And that's how it's meant to be. That's the cycle. But knowing it doesn't make it easier. There's still an ache. A small but steady hollow in my chest that fills with memories I don't always know what to do with.

I remember the way the house used to come alive. The early mornings with tiny feet pounding down the hallway, shrieking with joy. Wrapping paper flying, laughter echoing off the walls, someone always forgetting where they left the scissors. That frenzied kind of happiness, where the whole day sparkled with wonder.

Now, it's just a quiet morning and a cup of coffee for two.

But still—I try. I keep trying. I bake the pies. I hum along with old Christmas records. I wrap a few little gifts with tissue and ribbon, even if they're just for Tim and me. I light the candles. I set the table, even when no one's coming. I do it not for tradition's sake, but because these small gestures help me feel like I've still got a place in the story. Like I can still make a day feel special. Like Christmas still belongs to me in some way.

But once it's all packed away—once the final cookie is eaten and the last candle has flickered out—I find myself in that quiet place again. The days between Christmas and New Year's feel like stepping into a fog. Time moves differently. The air is thick with reflection and a touch of loneliness. It's a time no one talks about. The aftermath. The letdown.

The commercials switch to weight-loss goals and storage solutions, as if we can organize away the emotional weight we carry into January. But I feel it. That soft sadness. That quiet ache that doesn't ask for much, just to be acknowledged.

CHAPTER 13

The house feels different. Not sad, not empty—but quieter. Like it's resting after holding so much joy. And sometimes, I find myself resting too. Sitting with a blanket across my lap, watching snow fall through the window, a single candle lit beside me just to say, *I'm still here.*

Tim will be nearby, reading or dozing in his chair. We'll share the quiet like a prayer, each breath a small offering to the ordinary days ahead. Sometimes, I glance at him and feel overwhelmed with gratitude. Because in a world where so much has changed, he's still here. We're still here. And that is no small miracle.

I do miss the chaos. I won't pretend I don't. I miss the noise and the mess and the warmth of a full house. I miss the little voices and the way Christmas used to feel like an event instead of an echo. But I also know that those memories aren't gone. They live here, in these walls, in the photos I tucked into the corners of the mirror, in the ornaments with peeling paint and glitter fingerprints.

Now, Christmas is one pair of slippers by the door. One plate of leftovers. One candle lit at the table. And that's enough.

This new season of life—it's softer. Smaller. It comes in subtle ways. In the way Tim warms up the car for me before we go to church. In the way I still put extra cinnamon in the oatmeal on cold mornings. In watching an old black-and-white movie while curled up under the same quilt we've had since the kids were little. It's in the quiet that I've started to see the beauty that used to hide behind all the noise.

And yes, sometimes I still cry. I cry when I see an ornament that belonged to my mother. I cry when I hear a Christmas song that used to play while I rocked my babies. I cry when I make a roast and instinctively pull out enough potatoes for five instead of two. That grief never really goes away. It just grows quieter, like everything else.

But here's the truth I've learned in the stillness: Quiet holds healing, too.

It's in the quiet that I remember who I am. A woman who survived more than she ever expected to. A woman who no longer needs applause to feel worthy. A woman who can sit at a table set for two and still feel full.

I still bake. I still light candles. I still decorate. But not because I'm trying to recreate the past. I do it because I want the house to feel warm—for me. For Tim. For the memory of the life we built. For the love that still lingers in the corners.

We don't do the holidays like we used to.

Once upon a time, it was all about making it perfect. The food, the decor, the presents—everything had to be just right. I exhausted myself trying to create a moment I thought would make everyone feel loved.

Now? I just focus on creating peace.

There's a certain kind of magic in a quiet house. In a home where nothing is expected and everything is cherished. A place where the lights may be few but they shine intentionally. Where the meals are simpler but made with just as much love. Where two people can sit across from each other and feel more connected than ever before.

One night, not long ago, Tim and I had our little Christmas dinner. Nothing extravagant. Just ham, roasted carrots, warm rolls, and pickled okra from the jar because that's the kind he likes best. I set the table with mismatched napkins and a single taper candle in the center. Soft music played in the background and the snow tapped lightly on the window.

Tim reached across the table, took my hand, and said, "Thank you for always making it feel special."

And I smiled.

Because I hadn't done much.

But somehow, it was still enough.

We're writing a new kind of holiday story now. One where the characters are quieter, the plot a little slower, the scenes more focused on warmth than wonder. And it's okay. In fact, it's beautiful.

CHAPTER 13

This season of life—the one after the hustle, after the house is empty, after the sparkle fades—it's not lesser. It's just different. It asks different things of you. It invites you to find joy in smaller places. A good cup of tea. The soft glow of a lamp. A flannel robe. The sound of someone breathing beside you in sleep.

There's grace in the ordinary. And sometimes, I think grace is the point.

I still miss the noise, sometimes. The chaos. The crowds. The cheer. But I don't miss who I used to be in the middle of all that—tired, worried, pulled in too many directions. I've found a new kind of peace in this version of life. A steadiness. A sense of enough.

And so, when the decorations go away and the silence settles in, I no longer fear it. I embrace it. I breathe it in. I let it wrap around me like a familiar sweater.

Because this quiet?

It is not empty.

It is full of presence. Full of love. Full of healing.

And maybe, just maybe, it's the most sacred part of the season.

Chapter 14

If you had told the girl I once was that she would still be here—standing, breathing, healing, loving—she might've smiled politely but not believed you. Not fully. Not deep in her bones where the fear lived. Not in the places that still winced at kindness because it always came with strings. Not in the parts of her that had learned to expect pain before peace.

It wasn't that she didn't *want* to believe. She did. Hope was the tiny flicker she carried through the darkest hallways of her life. But she'd been through so much that imagining a soft landing felt like a luxury she couldn't afford. Because when life teaches you to brace all the time, it's hard to loosen your grip on the edge of the world.

And my life? It was a long stretch of holding on for dear life.

There was the childhood of noise and chaos. A father who didn't just raise his voice—he raised fear in the air like smoke, choking out the light. I remember nights when I'd lie in bed, gripping the blankets tight, staring at the shadows on the ceiling while my mother cried downstairs. Sometimes it was yelling. Sometimes it was silence that cut deeper than screams. And sometimes... it was the sound of something breaking. A plate. A door. A promise.

Home wasn't a place of rest—it was a place where you tiptoed, where you read moods like weather, where you kept your shoes by the door in case you needed to run.

CHAPTER 14

I grew up in survival mode. My nervous system learned to live on edge, ready to defend, ready to disappear.

And then there was *that* night.

I was still just a girl. Just starting to figure out who I was. Still sleeping with stuffed animals. Still not quite understanding how the world could be so cruel to a child who hadn't done anything wrong.

When it happened—the violation, the moment my world cracked in two—it wasn't loud. It was quiet. Terrifyingly quiet. And maybe that's what made it worse. There were no sirens. No rescue. Just me, alone with the shame I hadn't asked for.

That night stole something. Not just innocence. Not just peace. But the ability to rest without fear. The ability to *be* without hyper-awareness. The ability to *exist* without flinching.

And as if that wasn't enough... it happened again.

At fourteen, the world turned on me in a way I still struggle to wrap my head around. Assaulted again—this time by someone older, someone trusted. And when I needed my community, my neighborhood, my classmates—they didn't come close.

They turned away.

Worse—they turned *against* me.

They called me names. Whispered behind my back. Some didn't even bother to whisper. They made sure I knew I wasn't believed. That I wasn't worth protecting. It wasn't just the assault that hurt—it was the rejection that followed. That deep, burning realization that people will side with the one who looks less "inconvenient."

The girl I was disappeared after that. I tried to keep going. Tried to keep breathing. But every breath felt like a battle. And eventually... I left school. Left home. Left what little belief I had that life could be good.

Motherhood came next. And it was beautiful. And holy. And it *saved* me in ways nothing else could have. But it also wore me thin. I gave everything I had to my children, even when I didn't have much left for myself.

And still... the pain followed me.

One relationship after another. One more promise broken. One more bruise to cover. One more accusation. One more moment of being told, "You're not enough," or worse—"*You're too much.*"

There was that one night I'll never forget. Pregnant, bruised, holding my baby on one hip while being screamed at—timed on how long I took to get milk from the store. Watched constantly. Mind twisted by someone who wanted power over me.

And the gun.

That cold metal. That *click*. That moment where I didn't know if I'd live to see morning.

But I ran. In the dark, in fear, with nothing but my babies and a heart pounding so loud I thought it might give us away.

I found a shelter. I found strangers who believed me more than some of my own family ever did.

And then came the diagnoses.

PTSD. Severe depression. Bipolar. Schizophrenia.

They handed them to me like labels, like warnings—*as if I didn't already know I was different.* As if I hadn't already lived the symptoms. As if names could fix the damage.

But they did give me something else: medication. And that medication, while necessary, changed everything. My emotions. My sleep. My energy. My weight. My ability to feel like *me*.

I gained over 100 pounds. Stopped recognizing myself in mirrors. Stopped wanting to be seen. Stopped showing up in photos. I felt like a ghost in my own skin. Someone my past self would've never recognized. And some days, I was okay with that. Because invisibility felt safer than being seen and hurt again.

And then came the deepest cut.

My own son, angry and manipulative, became my guardian without me even knowing. Forced me into a prison inside my own home. Locked in my room, stripped of my dignity, plotted to have me institutionalized without my consent.

And it all could've happened if not for a tiny miracle. A cell phone I forgot I even had. A single percent of battery. One desperate call to my brother.

"Help."

And he did.

He came. He saved me. But the damage had been done.

My home was emptied. My things stolen. My heart gutted. I ended up sleeping in my mother's home. The same mother who had always put me last. Who would soon betray me in ways I never expected.

But that's also when everything began to shift.

Because that was the month Tim entered my life.

A friend request I'd forgotten. A comment. A number. A message. And just like that, something *gentle* came into the chaos.

He didn't come in loud. He didn't try to fix me. He just listened. He just stayed.

He took a bus from Alabama and moved in without even knowing what he was walking into. And when I barely spoke to him for months, when I flinched at kindness and shut down at the smallest things—he stayed anyway.

And over time… I let him in.

And over even more time… I let *myself* back in.

That's when the real healing began.

In the kitchen. In bread rising. In the scent of cinnamon. In Sunday tea. In simple dinners. In soft music and warm light. In moments that were sacred in their ordinariness.

I learned how to breathe again. Learned how to find joy in the quiet. Learned how to feel safe in my own skin—even if it took years.

And yes… I let go of people who couldn't meet me where I was.

My mother. My oldest children. Those who refused to love the new me, the healing me, the me who finally said "no more."

There's still grief in that.

But there's freedom too.

I drive by the house I thought would be mine—the house filled with memories of my stepdad, holidays, my babies playing in the backyard. And I see the for-sale sign. And my chest aches. But I don't stop. I don't cry. Not anymore.

Because I'm still here.

And I've built something softer. Something better.

A life where I don't flinch at the sound of the oven timer. A life where I play music just because. A life where I light a candle in the morning and smile at the scent. A life where I let love stay.

If you told the girl I once was that this is how it would turn out—she wouldn't believe you.

But I do.

Because I lived it.

I am living it.

And I'm still soft.

Still standing.

Still me.

* * *

There's something tender about the kind of gratitude that comes not from a good life—but from surviving a hard one.

It's not the loud, parade-style kind of gratitude. It doesn't show up in Instagram captions or shiny journals with gold-leaf lettering. No, it shows up quietly—like steam curling off a mug of tea after a long, weepy night. Like the soft thud of your own heartbeat reminding you you're still here.

That's the kind of gratitude I live with now.

I've come to believe the deepest kind of thankfulness isn't for the easy things. It's for the things that should've broken you... but didn't. It's for the parts of your life that nearly swallowed you whole, but somehow you crawled out with a little more softness instead of bitterness. That's a miracle in itself.

When I think about all I've walked through, it's almost hard to hold it all in one breath.

The trauma. The abuse. The betrayal. The diagnoses. The rejection from people who were supposed to love me best. And yet... when I lay my head down at night now, I find myself whispering, *thank you*.

Not for the pain.

But for what the pain *taught me*.

I'm grateful for what I've seen—because it gave me eyes that don't miss the small good things anymore. I notice them all now. The sunlight hitting the kitchen counter just right. The way Tim laughs at his own jokes. The feel of clean sheets when I slide into bed. The scent of vanilla and brown sugar curling through the air while something bakes in the oven.

These tiny things used to pass me by.

Not anymore.

Hardship makes you present. It slows you down. It rewires your brain to hold onto the gentle stuff because you've lived through the worst of it—and you know how fleeting peace can be.

I used to wish I had grown up different. I used to long for the kind of childhood I'd see on TV—picnics, bedtime stories, parents who protected and listened and showed up every time. I used to ache with jealousy at women who talked about their moms like best friends or shared old family recipes passed down with love. My childhood was a war zone. My home wasn't filled with laughter—it was filled with yelling, bruises, and broken promises.

But now? I can say this with no shame in my voice—I'm *grateful*.

Because that little girl who hid under the table to escape the screaming? She taught me resilience.

That girl who held her breath every time a door slammed? She taught me how to listen—to notice what's unspoken. To hear pain in someone's silence. That's part of why I can love Tim so well now. I notice what most people don't.

That teenager who was blamed and shamed and called names after being assaulted? She taught me the value of holding your head up, even when no one else believes you. She taught me that your truth is your truth, no matter who tries to silence it.

That young mom who escaped with nothing but her babies and her heartbeat? She taught me courage. She taught me the power of walking away even when your knees are shaking and you don't know what's waiting on the other side.

That woman in the hospital, in the psych ward, behind locked doors with a wristband that said *Danger to Self*? She taught me empathy. She taught me that healing isn't linear and people are fighting battles you'll never see. She taught me that there's no shame in medication, no shame in needing help, no shame in surviving however you need to.

I used to feel shame about all of it. Every diagnosis. Every failed relationship. Every time I had to start over. Every pound I gained. Every breakdown. Every sob into my pillow. Every time I said, "I'm fine," when I absolutely wasn't.

But now?

Now I see it all as *sacred*.

Every heartbreak carved space inside me to love deeper.

Every betrayal showed me how to spot real loyalty.

Every dark season taught me how to find light in the tiniest things.

CHAPTER 14

And I wouldn't be *this* woman—this soft, strong, open-hearted woman—if I hadn't been broken open again and again and *again*.

The brokenness made room for the beauty.

It slowed me down.

It taught me to cook slowly, with love in my hands. It taught me to organize my spices not because I *have* to, but because I *get* to. It taught me to brush my hair gently, with reverence, even on days I don't feel pretty. It taught me that lighting a candle in the kitchen before making dinner isn't silly—it's holy. It's intention. It's grace.

And the pain taught me how to find *God* in places I never expected.

Not just in church.

But in bread dough rising.

In quiet tea on the porch.

In the way Tim looks at me when I'm not wearing makeup and says, "You're beautiful."

In the way my hands still work. In the way my lungs still breathe.

The truth is, I don't regret any of it—not anymore.

Not even the worst days.

Because without the worst days, I wouldn't have recognized the best ones when they finally came.

I wouldn't have known what peace felt like unless I had lived through the storm.

And I *certainly* wouldn't have appreciated love if I hadn't first been mistreated and dismissed and silenced and betrayed.

Tim didn't just walk into my life like a hero. He walked in like a witness. Like a partner. Like a warm, solid place to rest my story without fear. And that love—it cracked open something in me I thought I had buried for good.

The part of me that still wanted softness.

That still wanted to give and receive love.

That still believed in *more*.

He never asked me to be better.

He never made me feel broken.

He just *stayed*.

And in doing so, he gave me something I'll be grateful for the rest of my life—a love I don't have to earn. A home where I can take off all my masks. A kitchen where we dance slow to oldies. A porch where the breeze feels like grace.

And I know not everyone gets that. I know there are people still waiting. Still healing. Still praying for something to hold onto. And if that's you, I want you to hear me when I say this:

I didn't think I'd ever be okay either.

But I am.

Not because everything got fixed.

But because *I kept going.*

And now I see all of it—the trauma, the tears, the tangled mess of my life—as *a sacred road.*

Not one I would've chosen.

But one I'm grateful for.

Because it led me here.

And here is beautiful.

Sometimes when I'm sitting at the kitchen table with my cup of tea, I'll look around our little home—the same home that used to feel like a place I had to fight to create peace inside—and I'll just *exhale*. Because I remember when the silence here used to scare me. When the tick of the clock made my shoulders tense. When I would jump if the furnace kicked on. And now? Now the silence feels like a soft blanket. Now the clock ticking reminds me I made it to another hour, another day.

Tim will often ask what I'm thinking about when he catches me staring off like that. Sometimes I tell him the truth. Other times I just say, "Nothing much." Because how do you explain that you're sitting in a chair you once curled into crying, and now you're simply enjoying the way the light comes through the curtain?

That's what gratitude looks like for me now. It's not fireworks and grand gestures. It's *noticing*. It's *feeling*. It's *showing up*.

I'm grateful for the days I don't cry. Grateful for the days I *do* cry, too, because they no longer scare me. I know the tears won't swallow me whole anymore.

I'm grateful for my body—even though I'm still learning how to love it. It's been through so much. It's held fear. It's held children. It's carried me through hospital doors and long walks through grocery store aisles when I didn't want to be seen. It's stood in courtrooms. It's curled up on the bathroom floor. It's baked bread and scrubbed floors and carried weight, both literal and emotional, for decades. And still—*still*—this body gets up with me each morning.

And maybe the thing I'm most grateful for is this: I'm no longer looking for someone else to save me.

I used to pray for rescue. For someone to swoop in and fix it all. But now I know—that someone was always me.

Yes, I have Tim. And yes, his love has changed my life. But *he didn't save me. I did.* I saved myself every time I got out of bed when I didn't want to. Every time I packed a lunch, folded a shirt, lit a candle, turned on the music and baked something sweet just to make the air around me feel gentle again.

I saved myself when I chose to stay soft in a world that told me to harden. When I told the truth even when it hurt. When I left when it would've been easier to stay. When I stayed when it would've been easier to run.

I saved myself with every whispered prayer.

With every time I let go of someone who didn't know how to love me.

With every meal I cooked not because I had to—but because I could.

There is gratitude woven into the very fibers of this life now.

Not a single moment of it has come easy. But I wouldn't trade this peace I have now for anything in the world.

There's gratitude in the way Tim pours my coffee before I even ask.

There's gratitude in the way our home smells like cinnamon and lemon most days—simple, cozy, warm.

There's gratitude in the way I can sit down and write this story without shaking. I used to tremble at the memories. Now I honor them. Now I see them as pieces of the map that led me home.

And there's gratitude in the fact that I'm no longer trying to win anyone's approval. Not my mom's. Not my grown kids'. Not the family members who couldn't—or wouldn't—see me. I spent decades bending and contorting myself to be loved. Now, I just *am*. I'm no longer trying to be the daughter, mother, or woman they expect. I'm just being *Jana*.

And that's enough.

I sit in this quiet life with my cup of tea and my cinnamon rolls and the man I love, and I think... *maybe this was always the goal.* Not success. Not perfection. Not a picture-perfect life. But this—this peace. This stillness. This ability to breathe without flinching.

This feeling of home.

It doesn't mean I don't still carry the scars. Of course I do. But they don't define me anymore.

Now they just remind me of who I *was*.

And how far I've come.

* * *

It's a soft morning—one of those where the light seeps through the curtains like it's trying not to wake you too quickly. The kind of morning where the warmth of the air wraps around you gently, like a quilt that's been warmed in the dryer. Everything feels suspended in time, slow and sacred. I stand in the kitchen, bare feet on the cool linoleum, the hum of the fridge the only sound keeping time. There's the faint smell of cinnamon and warm oats floating from the slow cooker I turned on before sunrise. And from somewhere outside, a single bird chirps. Just one. Like a small announcement: *You're still here.*

And I will be—God willing.

I picture myself years from now, maybe in my late seventies. My body slower, a little more stiff in the mornings, but my soul steadier than ever. There's something about aging that makes you less afraid of stillness. Less afraid of quiet. Maybe even a little in love with it. I imagine myself in the same little home Tim and I share now. The one with the chipped paint and creaky steps. The one we've filled with stories, soft music, and the kind of laughter that only two people deeply familiar with each other can share.

There I am, seated at the makeup table Tim built me long ago. My reflection in the mirror has changed—my face carries more lines, but none that I resent. Each one is a road map, a story, a survival. My long silver hair falls past my shoulders, soft and a little wild, like rivers of wisdom flowing down. I brush it slowly, reverently. Not out of vanity, but out of love. The kind of love you learn to give yourself after decades of denying it.

The same lace curtain hangs in the window. The same teacup sits in its saucer—chipped, but still beautiful. I've never been the type to replace something just because it isn't perfect. Some things are more beautiful because of their imperfections.

The world outside will have changed. There'll be new stores, new headlines, new worries. But not this room. Not this moment. This little corner of my world remains a sanctuary. Untouched by the chaos of the outside, it's held together by quiet rituals and soft devotion.

I like to picture us then—Tim and me. Still together. A little older. A little more bent at the edges. But full of that quiet love we built our life on. The kind of love that doesn't shout, but shows up. Every day. Love that remembers your favorite mug, rubs your back when your joints ache, and always pours the coffee just how you like it.

He'll walk in, slower than he used to, wearing that same worn-in flannel shirt he refuses to part with. I swear, the thing's practically falling apart, but he loves it. Says it feels like home. He'll glance at me in the mirror, smile like he always does, and say in that gentle voice of his, "You up already, love'?"

And I'll smile right back, brush in hand, and say, "Been up a while. Just enjoying the quiet."

Because by then, I'll have learned to treasure the quiet. To choose it. To sit in it without needing to be distracted.

We'll still have our little routines, like always. Breakfast will be eggs and toast, or oatmeal with brown sugar if I'm feeling nostalgic. Maybe pancakes on Sundays. And no matter what I serve, Tim will act like it's the best thing he's ever eaten. Even if I've made it a hundred times. That's just who he is. And maybe that's why I still love cooking after all these years—because he's never made me feel like it's something I *have* to do. Only something I *get* to do. Something I'm *good* at.

He'll drink his coffee with cream and lots of sugar. I'll have mine with cream and sweet and low. And we'll sit across from each other at the little kitchen table. Same spot, same sunbeam coming through the window. We won't say much. Maybe we'll listen to the radio. Maybe we'll just listen to the birds. But we'll be together. And that, to me, is church. Not the kind with pews or stained glass. But the sacred, steady kind of love found in the everyday.

Our home won't be fancy. It never has been. Maybe by then the roof will leak a little when it storms, or the linoleum will be peeling in the corner of the hallway. But we won't mind. We've never needed much. The walls are lined with stories. The floor holds the echo of old laughter and the shuffle of slippers in the morning. And even when the wind howls outside or the news gets heavy, our little home will be a warm place. A soft place.

CHAPTER 14

On weekends, I'll still bake something simple. Sweet rolls with orange glaze, or apple bread that fills the air with spice and warmth. Not because we need it, but because baking is my way of saying *I love you*. It's how I mark time. How I remember who I am.

Tim will fuss about the weeds in the yard, check the mail, maybe putter in the garage. I'll water the plants and talk to the squirrels like they're old friends. Maybe we'll keep a tiny garden—just tomatoes and herbs. Nothing too big. Just enough to keep our hands in the dirt and our hearts in the rhythm of the seasons.

I see us watching the world from our window. Wrapped in blankets. Cups of tea in hand. Watching snow fall or leaves swirl or the neighbor's kids run down the sidewalk. We'll laugh at how we've turned into the very old folks we used to smile at in the grocery store. The ones who knew how to slow down. Who understood the quiet.

And I'll thank God that I made it this far.

Because some days, even now, it still feels like a miracle.

I'll probably still check the locks before bed. Maybe more than once. Old habits die hard, especially the ones rooted in fear. I might still pause when a car pulls into the driveway unannounced. That fear—the one from long ago—it doesn't disappear. It just softens. Like a scar that doesn't hurt anymore, but still itches when it rains.

But even with all that, I'll be okay. Because I've learned how to carry peace in my pocket like a stone. I've learned that safety isn't always a place—it's a person. It's a rhythm. It's a life that makes room for you to breathe.

I picture candlelight at dinner. Even when it's just the two of us. Especially then. I'll serve something simple—maybe a beef stew and biscuits—and Tim will say, "This is real good," and I'll smile because I'll know he means it. And in that moment, I'll feel seen. Not for what I did, but for who I am.

I think that's the deepest kind of love—the one that sees you in the ordinary and still calls it beautiful.

And maybe by then, the past won't sting quite so much. Maybe I'll be able to drive by that old house without flinching. Maybe I'll have made peace with the versions of me that never got to be. Maybe I'll think of my mother and remember something sweet instead of something painful. Maybe I'll whisper a prayer of forgiveness—not for her, but for myself. For holding on so tightly to things I couldn't fix.

Because I've learned that healing isn't forgetting. It's learning to live with the remembering.

There's a vision I hold close—quiet and tender, one I visit often in my mind.

The house is calm. The sun is just beginning to set. That golden hour light drapes across the curtains, casting soft shadows across the room. The kind of light that doesn't ask anything of you. It just rests.

And in that light, I sit.

At my vanity, brushing my long silver hair. Each stroke of the brush a meditation. A moment of presence. A thank-you to the body that's carried me through all the years.

I look at myself in the mirror. Not with shame. Not with comparison. But with reverence.

Because I know now.

I know what she's been through.

I know what it took for her to be here.

Behind me, I hear the familiar creak of the floorboards. I don't even need to turn around.

It's Tim.

Same soft steps. Same slow smile.

"Still the prettiest woman I've ever seen," he says.

And I believe him.

Because love—real love—has a way of making you believe in things again.

CHAPTER 14

"Come sit with me," I say.

And he does.

We sit side by side. Two lives braided together by time, by shared days and shared healing. The silence is full—not empty. Full of everything we've lived through. Full of everything we've built.

And I think about the girl I used to be. The one who thought she'd never make it.

I send her love.

And I whisper, *Look what you've made it to.*

This quiet life.

This imperfect home.

This body, this heart, this breath.

This moment.

A life built of quiet things.

And as I sit there, the dusk folding itself around us like a warm blanket, I realize something—

This is it.

This is what healing looks like.

Not grand. Not loud. Not without scar or shadow.

But whole.

Honest.

Tender.

True.

And I smile.

Because I am home.

Because I am loved.

Because I am still here.

Closing Reflection

from the heart of Jana Rae

If you're still here, still holding this book, I want to thank you.

Thank you for walking with me through the shadows. For sitting beside me in the hard places. For allowing me to speak the things that for so long I kept tucked away. Writing this book wasn't easy. In fact, some chapters were written through tears, hands trembling on the keys, wondering if the words were too much—or not enough.

But I kept going, and I think maybe you did too.

Because there's something sacred in the act of surviving. And something even more sacred in telling the truth about it.

Maybe your story looks different than mine. Maybe it's still unfolding. Maybe you're still living in the middle of it, unsure where the next page will turn. But I hope you've felt it—between these lines, inside the ordinary, beneath the fear and grief and healing—I hope you've felt less alone.

We don't always get the closure we hoped for. We don't always get the apology. Sometimes we don't even get answers. But what we do get—if we keep showing up—is the chance to reclaim our lives, one small moment at a time.

A clean kitchen.

A quiet morning.

A hand to hold.

A second chance.

The world taught me to be afraid of my story. For years, I believed that brokenness made me less valuable, less lovable, less whole. But somewhere along the way, God began to whisper something different. He showed me that survival is not weakness—it's strength. That the scars I carry aren't shameful—they're proof that I lived. That I kept going. That I still am.

So if you, too, carry invisible weight... if you double-check the locks or sleep with the lights on or find it hard to trust the quiet—I see you. And more importantly, I believe in the version of you that's still becoming.

You don't have to have it all figured out.

You don't have to be "healed" to be worthy of peace.

You don't need to be fearless to be faithful.

There is so much beauty in choosing to stay. In baking bread while the world feels unstable. In lighting a candle even when the day feels dim. In building a soft life in a world that's been hard to you. These things matter. You matter.

And as for me—I'm still learning. Still healing. Still reaching for grace on the days when the past feels too close and the future feels too far. But I'm here. And so are you. And that means something.

So as I close this book, know this:

You are not alone.

You are not too much.

You are not broken beyond repair.

You are not forgotten.

And no matter what you've lived through...

You are still here.

Still breathing.

Still becoming.

Still unbroken.

With all my heart,
Jana Rae

Made in United States
North Haven, CT
17 August 2025

71792246R00111